Cambridge Elements

Elements in Creativity and Imagination
edited by
Anna Abraham
University of Georgia, USA

CONNECTIVE CREATIVITY

What Art Can Teach Us about Collaboration

Austin Choi-Fitzpatrick
University of San Diego

Gordon Hoople
University of San Diego

CAMBRIDGE
UNIVERSITY PRESS

Shaftesbury Road, Cambridge CB2 8EA, United Kingdom

One Liberty Plaza, 20th Floor, New York, NY 10006, USA

477 Williamstown Road, Port Melbourne, VIC 3207, Australia

314–321, 3rd Floor, Plot 3, Splendor Forum, Jasola District Centre,
New Delhi – 110025, India

103 Penang Road, #05–06/07, Visioncrest Commercial, Singapore 238467

Cambridge University Press is part of Cambridge University Press & Assessment,
a department of the University of Cambridge.

We share the University's mission to contribute to society through the pursuit of
education, learning and research at the highest international levels of excellence.

www.cambridge.org
Information on this title: www.cambridge.org/9781009504980

DOI: 10.1017/9781009505017

When citing this work, please include a reference to the DOI 10.1017/9781009505017

First published 2024

A catalogue record for this publication is available from the British Library

ISBN 978-1-009-50498-0 Hardback
ISBN 978-1-009-50500-0 Paperback
ISSN 2752-3950 (online)
ISSN 2752-3942 (print)

Connective Creativity

What Art Can Teach Us about Collaboration

Elements in Creativity and Imagination

DOI: 10.1017/9781009505017
First published online: October 2024

Austin Choi-Fitzpatrick
University of San Diego

Gordon Hoople
University of San Diego

Author for correspondence: Austin Choi-Fitzpatrick, achoifitz@gmail.com

Abstract: The story we often tell about artists is fiction. We tend to imagine the starving artists toiling alone in their studio when, in fact, creativity and imagination are often relational and communal. Through interviews with artistic collectives and first-hand experience building large-scale installations in public spaces and at art events like Burning Man, Choi-Fitzpatrick and Hoople take the reader behind-the-scenes of a rather different art world. This Element leverages these experiences to reveal what artists can teach us about collaboration and teamwork and to focus in particular on the importance of embracing playfulness, cultivating a bias for action, and nurturing a shared identity. This Element concludes with an invitation to apply lessons from the arts to promote connective creativity across all our endeavors, especially to the puzzle of how we can foster more connective creativity with others, including artificial minds.

Keywords: art, collaboration, collective, creativity, community

ISBNs: 9781009504980 (HB), 9781009505000 (PB), 9781009505017 (OC)
ISSNs: 2752-3950 (online), 2752-3942 (print)

Contents

1 The Literature: Art as Collective Action

Most of what we know about imagination and creativity in the arts comes from close studies of artists working hard to bring their gifts to the world. The result is a general sense that art is the product of individuals, and that artists are a special sort of person who see deeper or farther than the rest of us – secular prophets who take it upon themselves to motivate, chastise, inspire, and transform (Mulgan, 2023).

Popular culture often depicts the lone artistic genius, hard at work to bring their vision to the world through media like drawing, painting, performance, photography, printmaking, and sculpture. As a result, the individual artist sits both comfortably and alone in the cultural and conceptual spotlight. We have written this Element because we believe the individual artist is only one of several modalities through which a creative spark enters the world. Two brief caveats. First, we are writing primarily with sculpture and painting in mind, as other artistic genres, especially theater, film, and music, have already recognized the extent to which collaboration is crucial to their creative endeavors. Second, we are primarily in conversation with Western modes of creative practice. Much of what we recommend as a challenge to the status quo might very well be standard practice in other times and places. Nevertheless, our experience founding an artist collective suggests that a fixation on the individual artist overlooks the fact that regardless of locale, creative work is often relational. Art is frequently a feat of collective action.

For nearly a decade we have been collaborating on projects focused on how people collaborate. Gordon is an engineer and teaches in a school of engineering, and Austin is a sociologist who teaches in a school of peace studies. In our last project, we had Gordon's engineering students (often men who may go on to work for defense contractors) and Austin's peace studies students (frequently women who may want to join the Peace Corps) work together to build small drones and to discuss this technology's social implications. Fieldwork for that project led to a book about how teaching across big differences benefits everyone (Hoople and Choi-Fitzpatrick, 2020), and got us thinking about what kind of fruit other collaborations might bear.

Neither of us had this Element in mind when, in 2018, Gordon helped our colleagues to construct a large piece of art for an installation at Burning Man. The art event has grown, both in size and in the public's imagination, since starting as an ad-hoc gathering on a Bay Area beach in 1986 (Chen, 2009). Today, Burning Man brings together over 70,000 people in Nevada's Black Rock Desert each year. Neither of us had ever been, though the idea of a week invested in community, art, self-expression, and self-reliance intrigued us both. After another successful installation in 2019, we decided it only made sense for us to start a research project on collaboration in the arts, and for this effort to leverage our experience building things for Burning Man.

In the final analysis, this project involved extensive fieldwork, primarily in and around San Diego, California, as well as in Black Rock City. Our original empirical research, including interviews with twenty collaborative artists and more than 1,000 hours of participant observation, suggests that collaborations provide artists with shelter from the headwinds of markets, and a playground for experimentation. What's more, artistic collaboration builds community.

This combination of personal experience and novel data have led us to the conclusion that there are three conditions necessary for connective creativity to thrive: valuing play, having a bias for action, and cultivating a shared identity.

We believe these lessons are relevant to people who pursue creative and imaginative endeavors, regardless of whether they think of themselves as artists. Likewise, we believe our experience is relative to creative teaming efforts in other domains. This will not be surprising to anyone who has worked with others on a project in a laboratory, law firm, or on an assembly line.

This project's particular contribution to the social sciences is a case study of how *small groups organize to create art*. In our concluding section we suggest the importance of such collaborations is set to increase, as technology can exacerbate loneliness, while also offering opportunities to create alongside other, nonhuman, minds.

Small Cases Help Us Understand the Big Picture

Small Groups

Over the past few decades sociology, Austin's home discipline, has either zoomed in on individuals or zoomed out to focus on entire institutions and societies (Farrell, 2008). The world most of us actually spend most of our lives in – a world comprised of little clusters of people – is the one we sociologists tend to discuss the least. Sociologists are comfortable analyzing things like social movements, bowling leagues (or the idea of bowling leagues), nonprofit associations, corporations, or networks. But the groups we spend most of our lives in are quite a bit smaller than movements, corporations, networks, or institutions (to say nothing of macro categories like race, class, and gender). The ever-astute Gary Alan Fine (2012: 1) has referred to the little worlds we spend most of our lives in as *tiny publics*, those "discrete zones of action . . . that through their power in defining rights and privileges . . . fit into and constitute society." This approach echoes the work of earlier sociologists like Georg Simmel and Erving Goffman, each of whom spent their entire career focusing up-close on human interactions and small group relations.

Where the term *publics* imagines groups as the building block of *political* society, Fine makes it clear that most of what we call society happens at a more immediate level, and a good deal about how the world works, and why things change, can be better understood if we conceptualize all that activity as happening within groups.

Fine's work caught our eye because he's one of the few sociologists to conceptualize the ephemeral nature of the communities that gather for short periods of time in order to do something meaningful. In many ways this is how we feel about our experience building art *in* community here in California, and then installing that art *for* community at outsider art events (like Burning Man) and for everyone in public spaces.

In Fine's (2012) thinking, Burning Man can be thought of as a *macrogathering* (118), or a *wispy community* (118), or a *short-lived nation* (119). While groups are often small, Burning Man is a "*group* with a single perspective rather than as an inchoate mass" that offers a kind of *temporary citizenship*, "complete with local rhetoric, preferred behaviors, and moral order" (118). We have written this Element in order to puzzle through the implications tiny publics have on how we think about art.

Organize

The study of social movements exploded in the 1980s and has continued unabated. Nearly every day we hear news of people challenging the status quo, demanding that things change immediately (or stop changing altogether). Political scientist Sidney Tarrow has argued that protest tactics and movement vernacular are so ubiquitous, on the left as well as the right, in democratic as well as authoritarian regimes, that we live in *movement societies*. What explains movements? Over the last few decades scholars have reached a general consensus that collective action emerges when people decide there is an opportunity to act, and when they access the right resources, and when they leverage or create a collective identity (McAdam, 1999).

We're drawing implicitly on this approach. Artistic collaborations are the result of collective action. The work it takes to organize an artist collective is similar to the work needed to mobilize people for protests and social movements. Whether people are coordinating to create art or to change hearts and minds, there must be some agreement that now is a good time to do something, either because they believe that a window of opportunity is opening in a promising way or is threatening to close. People also need to trust that there are, or will soon be, resources sufficient for the task at hand. It's hard to build art without materials, without a space to collaborate and create, and without any way to get your art to the place where it will be displayed. And, finally, people want to feel like they are part of something, that the creative group has a collective identity, a sense of *we*-ness.

Create

What does it matter that this Element is about tiny publics organizing to create *art*? Sociology's attention to the *social* offers a strong starting point for any inquiry into connective creativity (this approach can be contrasted with psychology, where the individual is the primary unit of analysis).[1] As a result, we draw insight and inspiration from scholarship on the profoundly social and relational nature of creativity.

Central to a sociology of creativity is the assumption that creativity is a collaborative enterprise and a collective accomplishment. Individual creative efforts are situated in larger circulations of ideas and resources (Becker, 2008), filtered through class and status (Bourdieu, 1984), and subject to scrutiny from external critics and markets (Lena, 2019; Wohl, 2021).

Artist collectives are an example of a group type that Michael Farrell (2001) has called a *collaborative circle*. Usually comprised of eight to sixteen people, working together over a period of a decade or two, Farrell argued that collaborative circles tend to have several stages, starting with formation, followed by rebellion against authority, then moving to negotiating a new vision, engaging in creative work, undertaking collective action, experiencing separation, and finally having a nostalgic reunion. Over time, specific roles emerge, including gatekeeper, scapegoat, devil's advocate, and boundary marker. Once trust is established, creative breakthroughs often emerge from pairs of collaborators working together on particular aspects of a project.

The fact that collaborative circles are embedded in networks shapes the way novel cultural materials emerge and diffuse. Michael Farrell argues that literary innovation comes from small groups at the edges of creative networks while Randall Collins (1998) suggests that philosophical innovation comes from small groups positioned at the center of intellectual networks. Where Farrell's approach suggests that it is hard to be creative when we are surrounded by the status quo, Collins' framing indicates that it is easier to be creative when we are surrounded by cutting-edge knowledge, and easier to diffuse new findings from the center of a network. Thomas Rochon (1998) proposes that new ideas are hot

---

[1] The American Psychological Association defines Creativity as "the ability to produce or develop original work, theories, techniques, or thoughts. A creative individual typically displays originality, imagination, and expressiveness. Creative thinking refers to the mental processes leading to a new invention or solution to a problem. Products of creative thinking include new machines, social ideas, scientific theories, artistic works, and more." – www.apa.org/topics/creativity.

housed in institutions like universities and then handed off to social movements who take them to the streets and eventually into the halls of power.

This Element contributes to these conversations through an examination of how creativity works in artistic collectives. These groups are important, if overlooked, sites of cultural production. They also represent small communities – tiny publics – in and of themselves. As will become clear as the story unfolds, these individual instantiations, taken together, constitute a world of practice that lies outside the mainstream. We think of this as a renegade, or *maverick* art world.

Creativity and Imagination Are Relational

Is there such a thing as connective creativity? Asking this question requires us to step back and assess common assumptions of creativity. We love the sharp contrast Gerhard Fischer and Florian Vassen (2011) draw between two ways of thinking.

> YES. All creativity is collective. No creative person exists in isolation; all human beings, artists and scientists in particular, depend in their work and in their creative self-expression on the contribution of others. The original Western philosophical model of creative enquiry is the Socratic Dialogue: without question no answer (which in turn provides a new question). For philosophers like Martin Buber, the creative dimension arises from what lies between I and Thou. In Mikhail Bakhtin's literary theory, too, the creation of meaning can only proceed in dialogic interaction. Furthermore, all artistic creation aims at outside presentation and recognition in a process of collective reception.
>
> NO. Creativity is always individual. While the social dimension of the Artist's and the scientist's work is undeniable, it must nevertheless be stated that the original creative impulse, the intellectual spark that leads to innovation, can only ever be found in the individual mind. The original aesthetic model of this concept is the Romantic Poet: alone and at one with nature. While artists may be surrounded by collaborators and while the technology of some artistic or scientific production requires a highly complex team effort, the final work is always recognizable by the expression that an individual personality has stamped upon it.

This contrast is of course stylized. Yet it also challenges a widespread assumption about the nature of creativity and imagination.

Our argument is simple: Imagination and creativity always involve a back and forth between entities.[2] As we use the term here, imagination describes concepts and ideas that live inside an individual mind. This point is important to

---

[2] This Element builds on efforts to advance a relational approach to social theory, especially in the work of Georg Simmel (2009[1908]), Martin Buber (1970[1923], and Mustafa Emirbayer

emphasize, since it means something new can emerge inside the individual mind and never leave, unless the person doing the imagining pushes the ideas out into the world so that others can experience it.

At the most fundamental biological level, thinking is the result of neurons firing. We can think of imagination as the result of fresh connections in response to stimuli (new or old). Sometimes the stimuli are internal to the individual mind. We try to reconcile dissimilar thoughts. We attempt to resolve contradictions. Austin has found that he can learn things from himself if he talks out loud, as his mind furnishes him with ideas he didn't know he had, or with connections he had not previously made. Gordon can imagine a new idea for a sculpture, but strangely enough he doesn't know what it actually looks like until he sits down at his computer and starts to tinker.

Sometimes the stimuli for imagination, therefore, are external to the individual mind, as we engage with other people and the world. We learn something that contradicts a prior assumption. Our imagination sparks as we speak with and listen to others. The two of us have found the same thing happens when we are speaking with one another. We learn from one another, but also about ourselves, as we converse. Our imaginations are also sparked as we move sensorily through the world, smelling, tasting, feeling, listening, and seeing.

Imagination is a critical background condition for creativity (Abraham, 2018, 2020). It is hard to be creative if we have no imagination, and it is hard for others to understand what we imagine if we don't explain or show it in some way. Creativity is imagination spilling out into the world, and as a basic capacity everyone has, it should be nurtured whenever possible.

Individual creativity is one way the individual act of imagination takes form in the world. We have a new idea, an idea that is new to our mind, and we take action to bring it out. Action almost always takes the form of tangible speech or action. We make new sentences, we sketch new designs, we move our body in new ways, we reposition the tripod, we reorder the furniture. The artistic process can be thought of at two levels. First, and at the most basic chemical level, creativity within an individual's mind is occurring *between neurons*. Second, at the most basic social level, the idea is moving from the mind to speech, text, or action.

Connective creativity is the product of individual imaginations working together to bring something fresh and tangible into the world.[3] This process is fundamentally relational, insofar as individuals need to *work together*. The

---

(1997), and Emirbayer and Matthew Desmond (2015) and explored in other work by Choi-Fitzpatrick and Watkins-Smith (2021).

[3] "An approach of creative activity that emerges from the collaboration and contribution of many individuals so that new forms of innovative and expressive art forms are produced collectively by

motives for collaboration are many – camaraderie and a shared desire to spend time together, necessity and the need for many hands, or precedence and a sense of how things are done. The pattern of collaboration is clear. It is a process that plays itself out over time, as minds mingle, merge, diverge, reconverge around sketches and models and descriptions and trials and errors, and on and on.

Artistic artifacts are the result of four activities. First, something must be imagined. Second, the concept in the imagination must be moved from the world of imagination (inside a mind) to the world, via sketches, words, or models, so the thing might be better apprehended by others. Third, the artistic artifact must be created. Fourth, the artist artifact is then shared with the world, often with a bit of description about the concept and the materials. These four activities do not line up in simple linear fashion, as four chronological steps from imagining to sketching to creating to describing. Instead, the process is circular, with frequent recursions and returns and stops and starts only to find oneself back at the beginning.

Regardless of sequencing, the conventional model often leaves us with the impression that doing art involves a single person doing all four of these things. Our experience suggests that artists are not consistently expected to perform the third activity: Others may do the work required to bring the artifact into the world as long as the artist maintains control over the other activities.

A sculptor's design might be so sophisticated that it requires a specialized artisan to execute. But even in practices where the artist is more closely associated with the act of creation, a division of labor might, we can imagine, result in a situation in which a *painter* sketches the image and selects the paints, leaving it to a junior artist to finalize the details. The famed Flemish painter Peter Paul Rubens (1577–1640) managed a studio comprised of specialists skilled in particular areas – the depiction of animals, for example. The piece wouldn't be *a Rubens* until the lead artist signed the piece. In this way Rubens brought many people "under the signature" of the artist (De Wachter [2017: 9], and see also Fischer and Vassen [2011] and Stimson and Sholette [2007]). Jennifer Lena (2019) has noted the importance of the "*tombstone text* (the work's title, medium, dimensions, and the creator's name and birth and death dates)" in conveying significance. Michel Foucault (1984) called this the "author function." Most art worlds behave as if the idea, the framing, the sketching out, and the storytelling after the fact are what makes one person *the artist*.

---

individuals connected by the network. Connective creativity occurs when social interactions lead to new interpretations and discoveries which individual thinking could not have generated" (Fields, 2021).

Austin, with an undergraduate degree in photography, is convinced the same thing can be said of photographers like Gregory Crewdson and the late Erwin Olaf, both known for their large-scale photo shoots, which often require a large production team, perhaps also including a person whose particular job it is to press the shutter (as well as technical specialists to print up the final image). Crewdson (2008) has said that he never holds the camera, as he's not particularly comfortable with them.

Artistic collaborations often reverse the logic of the signature – implicitly or explicitly – to spread artistship and credit across multiple people, oftentimes in a way that splits where mainstream attention to individual artists lumps. Sometimes, as in our own artistic practice, described in Section 3, the signature is absent altogether.

In other words, these tasks needn't be confined to a singular creative self. Our experience has convinced us that, in connective creativity, *the artistic artifact is an emergent property of collective action*. Individuals are creative, but it is usually only by working with others that our creativity is manifested in the world. Singular accomplishments by a singular creative self are both possible and potentially transcendent. They are also perhaps rarer than late capitalism's art worlds and artists admit.

Connective creativity, therefore, produces an idea or artifact that would not have been created otherwise, had a single mind operated alone on the task. The result is something that no one person can lay claim to. Of course, iterative processes are not exclusive to collectives. Instead, emergence is a simple by-product of collaboration and teamwork, and is precisely how a great number of fresh ideas are kicked around and cobbled together as they bounce between minds. We suspect this process is how a great deal of individual-level creativity finds its way from imagination, into conversation, back to reflection, and in this way iteratively evolves into a cultural artifact that the singular creative self takes credit for.

Whether the unit of analysis is an individual imagination, an individual act of artistic creativity, or a group's connective creativity, we are focused on the *relational* nature of the process. This approach deserves attention for several reasons.

Relationally, and in the nearest term, we face a truly global mental health crisis, driven by many factors, but especially the fact that new technologies (especially social media) have simultaneously increased individual imagination and creativity while nearly destroying actual human connection and collaborative engagement. People need to create. People need to connect. We need to find ways to do that if we want our societies to flourish. We need tiny publics.

In the medium term, other kinds of minds are coming online with which we can collaborate. The ability to spark creativity by bouncing nascent ideas off another mind is expanding, thanks to advancements in "artificial intelligence." The ability to work alongside artificial minds in the creation of novel text and images ushers in a new era of collaboration, though it is rarely thought of in these terms. Our approach to imagination and connective creativity thus applies to nonhuman minds as well.

In the longer term, we believe that humanity is at a critical juncture. Looming changes in geopolitics, climate, energy, geopolitics, science, and technology will increase challenges related to poverty, migration, inequality, conflict, and planetary habitability. Humanity cannot afford to outsource creativity to technologies. We must democratize and accelerate the process of creating new ideas and institutions that ensure all life flourishes.

If repair and renewal are imperative, and if capitalism is not up to the task, then fresh ideas are needed. Societies, like industries, need places to experiment and play. We need research and development for the public good. The arts, like social movements, think tanks, and universities, are places where society does some of its freshest thinking. One of the reasons we started an artist collective, and wrote this Element, is that we don't believe things will get better if we simply wait around to see what fresh ideas roll out from the engineers in America and China, or from Silicon Valley and Wall Street. The transitional next decades require large-scale investments in democratizing connective creativity for the common good.

Our view of the creative process – *in relationship and over time* – offers refreshing opportunities to create and build together, in the present moment, in the medium term, and at the macro-historical level.

Art Worlds Are Relational

Artistic artifacts emerge from a host of conventions, are supported by a host of actors, are sponsored (or not) by patrons, displayed (or not) in galleries, and received (or rejected) by audiences, critics, and collectors.

The entirety of what makes a particular artifact *art* and a particular person an *artist* is described by sociologist Howard Becker as comprising an Art World. Ever the consummate ethnographer, Becker was at various times in his life a jazz musician as well as a professional photographer. Becker defines an "art world" as a network of people who cooperate to make, evaluate, and circulate works of art. These webs of social relationships create various roles for creatives. These include the *integrated professional artist*, who is deeply embedded in the traditional art world and adheres to its norms. These are the artists whose work can be found in leading galleries and collections, whose faces can be found on trade publications, and whose presence can be expected at the right kinds of cultural gatherings. Integrated professionals, in Becker's conceptualization, are the consummate insiders. They look like one imagines an artist should look. Their work is widely thought of as art. They have arrived, and the location of their arrival is the mainstream art world.

Becker compares these integrated insiders with Folk artists, creators who are part of a community's cultural heritage and who create artistic artifacts that reflect traditional practices and traditional values. They tend to do this wherever they are, with little reference to mainstream art worlds. Likewise, *naive artist* is Becker's term for self-taught creators, whose work is characterized by a raw and authentic expression. The naive artist is unconstrained by formal rules, and their work exists completely independent of mainstream art worlds. Where integrated artists are, by definition, *integrated into* the mainstream, naive and folk artists lie outside the mainstream, lacking any relationship to important centers of production.

We wrote this Element in order to draw attention to an important fourth category of artist: Mavericks. *Maverick artists* are renegades who go about their work fully aware of what the mainstream entails and requires. They understand the trends and rules prevalent in the centers of production, but, for whatever reason, they have chosen to work outside them. Mavericks, as it turns out, often pioneer avant-garde practices. Occasionally, the rebellious novelty produced by such an artist makes its way toward the center, into the canon, and into the status quo.[4]

What, exactly, are integrated artists working in relation to (and, conversely, what are mavericks rejecting altogether)? Beyond the artists lies a constellation of critics, gallery owners, collectors, curators, and other individuals and institutions involved in the art scene. An art world is not a single, monolithic entity but rather a complex and interconnected web of social relationships that interact and contribute to the creation and maintenance of the art world's shared conventions and practices. Even the solo painter holed up in an attic, emerging only once a year to deliver paintings to a gallery, requires an entire ecosystem – materials, brokers, critics, buyers, bookkeepers, assistants, enemies, and so on – to ensure the work enters the world in a way that it can be seen, acquired, and appreciated.

This lesson applies even to an artist as iconoclastic as Vincent van Gogh, who has as legitimate of a claim as any to being a singular creative entity, and whose

---

[4] This situation describes 3B Collective, who we meet later. Social movement trends pushed their social justice-related work into the limelight. This created fresh tensions, as when the artists, most of whom are Chicano, show up for a gallery installation and can see gallerists apprising the crew, perhaps wondering to themselves *when can we expect the artist?*

ecosystem was small, but not nonexistent. It is difficult to imagine materials getting into van Gogh's hands, and the art making its way out of his cramped quarters, were it not for Vincent's brother, Theo. Becker's skill lies in demonstrating how these conventions influence the creation of art and how changes in an art world can occur.

What's more, Becker's approach suggests that the singular form – art *world* – is inaccurate, as there are many such networks of support, supply, demand, approval, and so forth. There are, in fact, Art *Worlds*. We can confidently say that fine art comprises one art world just as surely as anime comprises another art world. Seen in this way, artwork is an accomplishment made possible by the many actors and actants who live within a particular art world, or creative ecology. As we have already seen, there is a large body of scholarly evidence for the ways networks, groups, tiny publics, and collaborative circles make creative breakthroughs possible, while also demonstrating the way these changes interface with the broader political, social, economic, technological, and ecological environs they are situated within.

All art is a collective accomplishment, but the world is unforgiving. The nature of art markets, the financialization of art, capitalism, inequality, individualism (and perhaps also vanity) suggest the smartest thing for an artist to do is to hone their style, sharpen their identity, and build their brand. Sharing credit with the broad cast of characters Becker summons onto the stage is foolish if time is short and the rent is due. The result is isomorphism, and an underlying conformity as a creative person learns to perform as an integrated professional, who now belongs to an important art world's mainstream.

Acting like you belong involves nurturing the idea that all artists, and most all of one's work, are the result of a singular creative self, an especially gifted individual with a unique cultural role and identity. Artists have egos and social standing, surely, but they also correctly ascertain the importance of manufacturing an identity, especially in the face of external pressures faced by all workers in late capitalism.

The story of the solitary genius is pervasive, and it rewards high-status stars, not low-ego collaborations. Mainstream art worlds invest significant resources in the spaces, institutions, and norms that underwrite this status quo.

We are now in a position to better understand why this makes us uneasy. It's too simple. Even individual artists, Becker shows, are the product of rich systems and dense flows and extensive networks. At a minimum, we should recognize that individual artists are the result of situatedness in mainstream art worlds. We wrote this Element in order to highlight alternatives.

Collaborative Art Worlds

In a lovely book titled *Co-Art* (2017), the critic Ellen Mara De Wachter showcases her conversations with twenty artistic collaborations. She argues that cooperation is a *key driver of artistic creation*, but we tend to miss this fact, as art history has hued more to the great man theory of innovation and creativity, centering our gaze, wrongly, on an ideal type. She's right to imagine that "an alternative art history would involve an account of the constant interplay between the individual and the group" (p. 6).

One reason cooperation has been overlooked by Western historians, De Wachter suggests, is that the Cold War thinkers viewed collectives and avant-garde groups "with suspicion, their activities considered to be watered down versions of those performed by Eastern Bloc Communist organizations" (p. 7). But even this was an anomaly, Fischer and Vassen (2011) point out, since it wasn't until the Enlightenment, in the West at least, that calling oneself "a creator" would have been seen as anything other than blasphemy.

Howard Becker had it right: Individual artists are nodes in a network, rather than the top of a pyramid, or a lone flickering candle. Certainly, there is a center to the network, where some nodes are more central. Individual artists can be part of the mainstream (integrated artists). Or they can spend their days challenging the mainstream (mavericks and perhaps folk artists). Some are oblivious to the mainstream altogether (naive artists).

Artistic collaborations like those described by De Wachter, and here in this Element, are likewise situated in larger art worlds. A collaboration can be part of the mainstream (integrated collaborations), challenge the mainstream (maverick collaborations), or oblivious to the mainstream (naive collaborations).

Integrated collaborations can be found wherever a lead artist works with others, as seen in the case of Anish Kapoor, who we will meet later in this Element. Integrated collaborations, like integrated artists, might find themselves in the mainstream art worlds centered in a widely recognized metropolis, including Basel, Berlin, Los Angeles, London, Miami, New York, and Paris. These are home to the most prominent institutions, especially galleries, museums, and auction houses. It is also where many major critics and buyers are based.

If it is maverick *artists* who hold our attention, then we must inquire into the conditions that allow maverick connective creativity to flourish. Maverick collaborations, like maverick artists, are more likely to emerge at the periphery, in places like Bombay Beach and Joshua Tree, California, or Marfa, Texas, or to thrive in autonomous zones like Freetown Christiania in Copenhagen, Denmark.

The relentless onslaught of financialized capitalism ensures that all lists are partial. Had we written this Element twenty years ago we might have included Nashville, Tennessee, and fifteen years ago we might have mentioned Austin, Texas and Portland, Oregon and Brooklyn, New York. Today little remains of the maverick spirit each once hosted.

Conclusion

Contemporary art worlds are situated in late capitalism. Individual egos, financial pressures, and the demands of investors and consumers reward the cultivation of overly individuated narratives of artistic production. The individual artist reigns supreme in the public imagination. Yet even individual artists are enmeshed in art world fractals.

Art is best thought of as collective action. This is in stark contrast to the dominant myth of the singular creative self. The fundamental benefit of imagination and creativity lies in the opportunities they provide for community and connection. If we want to nurture these forms of collaborative practice, however, we need new forms of play and practice, new norms for valuing this work, and fresh institutional support. It deserves noting that we draw inspiration from Burning Man, a Maverick Collaborative Art World that varies dramatically in terms of credit, commerce, and intent from the integrated artists of the mainstream and status quo art world.

2 The Actors: Types of Artistic Collaboration

How should we think about artistic collaboration, especially in sculpture and painting? Our species is fundamentally creative. Clearly, our capacities and interests may vary and the extent to which society supports or hinders an individual's creative capacity is uneven.[5] While every one of us is an individual creative person, only some formalize this capacity and present themselves to the world as an *artist*. Of those who do embrace the artist identity, many spend their entire careers working on their own.

Some others, though, choose to collaborate, and it is the collaborative opportunities that hold our attention. In particular, we identify three broad categories of artistic collaboration. It is possible to think of these three forms on a continuum. At one end of the spectrum we have the *Lead Artist*, where we are told a single, definitive artistic voice brings together a group to execute a single unique vision. At the other end of the spectrum are *Artistic Collectives*, groups that philosophically eschew individualistic credit and identity in their

---

[5] Systemic factors include, for example, poor educational systems, environmental degradation, and pollution.

work and instead foster a group identity. In the middle of the continuum we find the *Artistic Collaboration*, where artists (who may have their own solo practices) come together to make art in a group, but choose not to subsume their creative identity in that collaboration. These categories are not mutually exclusive. A solo artist can have a thriving practice and a prominent name in the field, also be a prominent half of an artistic collaboration, *and* also be a partner in a collective.

The Individual Creative Self

Individual creative self is our way of talking about the fact that creativity comes from imagination, and imagination comes from the individual mind. Austin is convinced of the duality and relationality of all thinking, so inside the mind he wants us to imagine neurons firing off one another, in a synaptic cascade, or firing in response to stimuli from the outside world, such that *all thinking is relational.*

As a scholar of social movements, Austin is attentive to any instance in which people decide to imagine, initiate, or support alternatives to the status quo. The first step in pursuing change is recognizing that the status quo is problematic, and that fresh ideas and actions are needed. Creativity is needed for innovation in our political, social, and economic lives. Sociologist Hannah Wohl (2021: 1) has noted that "while creativity is a process, innovation is the outcome of this process." Indeed, we have creative individuals and groups to thank for every bit of what we see around us today (for better or for worse).

We want to increase the stock of positive creative capacity available in society. Thus, for us, creativity and imagination come in many forms. The political anthropologist James C Scott (2012) has suggested that in our everyday lives we should be practicing what he calls *anarchist calisthenics* – limbering up to act intentionally in the world, rather than sleepwalking. Jaywalking, for Scott, is an excellent case study of those moments when we can decide whether we want to take matters into our own hands.[6] The metaphorical alternative to jaywalking, Scott suggests, is sleepwalking.

Scott's logic can be seen in *social practice art*. Emerging over the last few decades, thanks to the work of well-positioned advocates like Tania Bruguera and Suzanne Lacey, social practice art is premised on community engagement. Drawing on participants, place, and relationship, this approach is focused less on the artistic artifact per se, organizing instead on the realization of new social orders (Bishop, 2012; Helguera, 2012; Thompson, 2012). The intended

---

[6] Of course, not everyone is able to jaywalk without fear of reprisal, as inequality punctuates policing worldwide.

resonance is not with formal art worlds and its trendlines, but instead with our experience of life's most intense contractions. In a write-up of the social practice art movement, the *New York Times* suggested the reader "Think Soviet agitprop, performance art and Bansky with the social consciousness of the community organizer Saul Alinsky" (Grant, 2016). The core lesson social practice art offers us here is that imagination and creativity are fundamental to change processes.

Imagination and creativity are also central to being real and alive people in the world. Our overarching philosophy owes a great deal to the philosopher Roberto Unger (2007), who has argued against the mistaken impression that we are products of the market, or servants of the state. While we may be born into a world in which the rules and institutions appear fixed, Unger argues, they are the result of desiccated human agency – they are the things left behind by earlier creative efforts by imaginative forebearers. States, markets, and societies, and the norms and institutions that make them possible, are the result of human imagination and creativity. *There is always more in us than is in the world*, Unger argues, making creativity and imagination the source of all we see. Humanity's birthright is to nurture, connect, create, and discover.

The Individual Artist

We are all capable of imagining and creating, but only some of us take the next step to identify as an *artist*. We use the term *individual artist* to describe a person who makes art by themselves. They come up with the idea, say for an image, and then using their own hands, or a brush, or a camera, or a computer, bring that idea into reality.

As seen in the previous section, such individual artists live within densely networked and thickly articulated art worlds that have their own currency, their own culture, their own rules, their own gods, their own ebbs and flows, and their own strictures and rewards.[7] Mavericks are notable because they eschew the mainstream art world.[8]

---

[7] Austin is reminded of the words of John W Borneman, the esteemed anthropologist. Austin was a PhD candidate and had begun presenting early results from his fieldwork at conferences, not just in his home field of Sociology, but also in Criminology, and perhaps most unwisely, at the American Anthropological Association on the year the conference was held in its native city of Chicago. Austin's paper was drawn from NSF-funded semi-structured interviews and focus groups – a respectable approach for sociology, but Borneman signaled how wide of the mark this methodological approach was by declaring: "Choi-Fitzpatrick you can come into our temple, but you cannot piss on our idols." Austin has long loved to tell this story, especially when asked *What makes a discipline a discipline?*

[8] Of course, Naive and Folk artists live outside art worlds entirely, by definition.

The clearest criterion for an individual artist is the proactive step required to convert the individual imaginative spark into a specific creative artifact. Art worlds assist in this transformation, more or less, and in various ways, but the artist works alone, perhaps for long stretches of time, up to and including entire careers. We have already argued that artistic artifacts are the fruit of four overlapping and recursive activities: (1) imagining the concept, (2) sketching or describing the piece, (3) building the piece, and (4) describing the piece to others.

The conventional model of the artist often leaves us with the impression that doing art involves one person doing all of these activities. Our experience suggests that artists are not consistently expected to actually do the work necessary to build the thing, but this Element is about what happens when people decide to do the work themselves, together.

The Lead Artist

A lead artist is a single individual who claims total creative control over a project. Unlike a painter in their studio alone with a canvas, however, the projects are often at a scale beyond what can be accomplished by a single person. This category includes contemporary artists such as Jeff Koons, Maya Lin, Tom Sachs, Yayoi Kusama, and Anish Kapoor. These artists are prolific – and sometimes controversial – as they leverage the power of groups to scale their work.

If you read a museum placard for a sculpture by Anish Kapoor, you'd be forgiven for thinking that the piece was made with the artist's hands alone in his studio. There's typically the title, his name, and a short description of the piece. Left unwritten is that these types of artworks are the result of collective action. Depending on the piece of art, there may be dozens or even hundreds of individuals who have had a hand in shaping the final product.

Kapoor's workshops encompass a city block in the Camberwell district of South London, with a different warehouse devoted to each of his signature fabrication processes. There he employs a team of thirteen technicians – each with incredible skills ranging from stone carving to welding – who help transform his sketches into artifacts. Lead technician Pablo Smidt has worked with Kapoor for nineteen years. And these are only his closest collaborators. For especially large or complex projects he collaborates first with engineers to create structurally sound designs and then contracts with construction companies to bring them to life. As gallery owner Greg Hilty explained in a *New Yorker* profile of Kapoor: "He has a group of people he has worked with for a really long time. And they know what he wants, and think what he thinks, to a certain degree. They have evolved with him, and they have helped him evolve his language" (Mead, 2022).

No one doubts that it is Kapoor who drives the creative process or that he is intimately involved in every step of production. As his lead technician explained: "He is not someone coming in here and giving directions and going away. When it is the moment to work, he works like anybody else – or more." Without this team, Kapoor's art would not be possible. It might be Kapoor who sketches an idea, but it is the technicians who spend months creating different scale models for him to choose among. And it is Kapoor's name on the museum's plaque.

This begs the question: Why is it Kapoor, lead artist, as opposed to The Kapoor Collective? While we won't hazard a guess on Kapoor's particular motives, broadly we see two major influences that drive artists toward the lead artist archetype as opposed to collectives: ego and markets.

First let's consider ego. *Ego* can cut both ways. In the best of times we can think of ego as nothing more complex than the human desire to be recognized for our work, for creative vision, and for what we offer to the world. Then there's the trappings of ego, the shadow. All too often we are tempted by a sense of self-importance, the propensity to exaggerate our abilities and achievements, and a temptation to claim credit for the work of others. This self-image can lead people to seek fame and the validation and admiration of others. Each of these traits align strongly with our concept of a lead artist.

Ego in either form, however, is not the only reason someone may choose to be a lead artist. The other, perhaps more powerful, incentive is the mainstream art world *market*. That market loves the story of a good lead artist. People want to believe the myth of the singular creator – the idea that one person is solely responsible for a piece of art. Many art buyers are looking not for a particular aesthetic, but instead seek the cache associated with owning a particular brand. This is one reason Kapoor has been able to sell hundreds of his signature mirrored disks – people want to own a part of this story and his brand. Students in Masters of Fine Arts (MFA) programs are explicitly trained to build their brand around a clear identity and a coherent body of work (Fine, 2018). This is capitalistic markets at work, incentivizing artists to create putatively unique personas (Lena, 2019).

Zooming out from the specific case of Anish Kapoor, we can turn our attention to the archetype of the lead artist and the unique set of skills and qualities it requires. These individuals must not only be adept at their craft but also possess the ability to navigate the complex dynamics of collaborative art creation. Successful lead artists excel in bringing together diverse talents and fostering a sense of loyalty among their collaborators. They must also be able to integrate diverse ideas, creating a cohesive vision that both reflects and disappears the collective effort involved in the artistic process. This skill is essential for orchestrating large-scale projects that go beyond the scope of individual effort. They also must be able to cultivate a public persona that resonates with the spirit of the times. This ability to capture the zeitgeist is crucial for establishing a brand and connecting with a wider audience.

Empowering highly creative individuals to leverage the power of groups has its merits. In the realm of artistic creation, the lead artist serves as a visionary orchestrator, capable of realizing ambitious projects that might lay beyond the scope of individual artists. Their singular vision, supported by the group they lead, is able to shape the entire arts ecosystem. Their ability to galvanize resources and talents creates a ripple effect that benefits not only the lead artist but also the collaborators and the broader artistic community.

This mode of practice, however, is not without its challenges. One significant risk is the potential for lead artists to inadvertently co-opt the ideas of others as their own. Power imbalances within the hierarchical structure can stifle the creativity of collaborators, hindering the free exchange of ideas and diminishing the diversity of voices in the artistic process.

The case of Tom Sachs, in particular, comes to mind. Sachs is a well-known artist who explicitly and intentionally operates his studio as a cult. Employees wear uniforms with serial numbers, are expected to place all items at parallel or 90 degree angles, and must adhere to strict diet-and-exercise regimes (Schneider, 2023). Most germane to our conversation here, the first of his ten rules governing employees is "Work to Code: Creativity is the Enemy."[9] This is a very different approach to being the lead artist than we saw with Kapoor.

What is most surprising about this category is that no one thinks about it. When people hear the name of a famous artist, they typically imagine an individual working alone in their studio, as we described in the previous section. In reality, any contemporary artist famous enough for most people to have heard about is probably much closer to what we describe here as the *lead artist*. While these folks have by and large cultivated an individual identity, the open secret is that they simply can't do their art alone, at least not at the scale required by capitalistic consumer society. They have a team supporting them – helping them to bring their vision into reality. How these teams are acknowledged and treated varies widely, as we see in the examples of Kapoor and Sachs. Here again ego and markets are the major players, determining just how public *lead artists* are willing to be about the team behind the artist.

---

[9] Sachs, Tom. "10 Bullets." December 6, 2010. Video. www.youtube.com/watch?v=49p1JVLHUos.

The Artistic Collaboration

Artistic collaborations, as we conceptualize them here, take the form of one-off, or extended, alliances *between individual artists*, each with their own identity, style, and practice. What sets collaborations apart is the way in which they involve cooperation between actors more accustomed, perhaps, to working without accompaniment. The collaboration, then, is often a suspension of the drive of ego and the pull of markets. Or, more likely, there is an opportunity presented by the market to engage in a "colab" or "feat" between two artists, such that each benefits from their proximity to the other.

Artists Sheena Rae Dowling and Yvette Roman met in 2016 while working for La Maestra Foundation, a nonprofit located in the City Heights neighborhood of San Diego, California. When Gordon asked them how their collaboration began, Dowling explained it was mostly happenstance:

> It was just kind of serendipitous that we happen to have similar interests, similar teaching practices, similar missions and goals. And in our creative process it worked out that we wanted to do projects beyond just what was being asked of us at the nonprofit.

Each of them had an established artistic identity and individual practice before their collaboration began. Dowling had earned an MFA in sculpture and a BFA in painting, while Roman earned her BA in Visual Arts. It was a nonprofit that brought them together, but their relationship grew beyond what was required by their employer. Their collaboration led to a shared interest in processing trauma. As Dowling explains:

> Our work has centered a lot on healing from traumatic experiences. Working with groups of people that have been impacted by really life altering events, and how we can use the arts to help process that and engage with that difficult territory.

The first major artistic endeavor they undertook together was *Collective Memory*, a public installation in a city park. This event-based installation aimed to recreate the ambiance of a sunny afternoon picnic while inviting the community to engage in a collective reflection on the experience of the COVID-19 pandemic. At the heart of the installation stood the Memory Dome, a tent-like structure providing an intimate space for individuals to process and share their experiences, emotions, and memories related to the pandemic.

Picnic blankets, crafted from fabric remnants and clothing donated by community members through prior workshops, encircled the central dome, creating an open space for socializing and communal engagement. Within the Memory Dome, text-based pieces, comprising recreated accounts and stories gathered from the community, hung on strips of fabric. Park-goers could freely enter and exit the dome, contributing to a collective narrative of grief, loss, hope, and joy.

When Gordon asked about the challenges of collaborating, the two women laughed. Clearly, they have great rapport and are like minded, but they admitted working together is not always easy. Dowling recalled one particularly tough choice around what material to use:

> We had a different picture in our brain even just as simple as the color of a fabric. How are we going to do this? ... How are we going to come to a place of compromise? ... How can I let go of my ego in order to stay behind the intention of this project?

A defining feature of the artistic collaboration is the willingness and ability to let go of sole creative control. These collaborations prioritize the comingling of ideas – each artist brings their own sensibilities, aesthetic, and vision to the project. This results in friction, as creative individuals accustomed to working independently suddenly find themselves forced to reckon with other imaginative and creative minds. When done well, this creative friction is enormously beneficial, yielding a product that neither artist would have conceived of on their own. As we heard from many of the other artists we spoke with, collaboration offered the chance to escape their own tightly constructed artistic narrative and see the world from a different perspective. The friction and fission are a virtue.

Artist Collectives

Artists collectives are in direct opposition to the *lead artist* model. Often on the fringe of mainstream art worlds, sometimes associated with social movements or political action, and never easy to categorize, collectives have a storied history. For our purposes in this Element, we narrow our definition of an artists collective to a group of artists who create work together under a *collective identity* that goes beyond any single group member.

Specifically, we differentiate this practice from the collaboration or lead artist models. An artist collective produces work that cannot be signed by any one person, but is instead cosigned by the entire collective, as it were.

The forms of practice taken by collectives are widely varied. Some collectives might include just two members, while others count their membership in the hundreds. Even the idea of membership itself is not consistent – some collectives maintain the same members over decades, while others have a constantly changing cast of characters.

Artist collectives, historically on the fringes of the mainstream art world, have recently gained prominence as institutions seek to embody social change.

We're thinking of the appointment of an Indonesian collective to lead an exhibit in Germany, and the appointment of a collective to direct the Viennese Kunsthalle. This shift suggests a possible decline in art-world individualism, underscored by collective appointments to prominent exhibitions and collective recipients of major prizes (Brown, 2023).

Conclusion

Imagination and creativity are our birthrights. The world is made and unmade when we put our ideas into action. This is especially true in uncertain times. Some people decide to be artists, and art worlds have many different types of actors, connecting and collaborating in various ways. At one end stands the lead artist, where a singular visionary claims total creative control, orchestrating a symphony of talents to bring forth a unique vision. These individuals possess not only artistic prowess but also the ability to inspire loyalty, integrate diverse ideas, and cultivate a public persona that resonates with the current moment. The lead artist archetype, while capable of realizing monumental projects, grapples with the challenge of potential idea co-option and power imbalances.

On the opposite end emerges the enigmatic world of artist collectives, where the boundaries of individualism blur, and collective identity takes precedence. Collectives range from small, steadfast groups to expansive, ever-evolving collaborations. Historically on the periphery of mainstream art worlds, collectives are experiencing a resurgence, challenging the dominance of individualistic narratives and gaining recognition as agents of social change. The next section introduces a case study of a collective's emergence from one-off collaboration.

3 The Case Study: ArtBuilds Collective

Introduction

This Element about connective creativity has been shaped by our experience creating a maverick artist collective. Put simply, our collective is the emergent property of cooperation. We did not set out with any particular intention other than having fun with like-minded people. The case study of the ArtBuilds Collective suggests one way in which individuals decided to collaborate, and how that collaboration evolved into a collective.

Unfolding Humanity: From Individual Creative Selves to Collaboration (2018–2022)

Our colleague Diane Hoffoss is a math professor at the University of San Diego, where we teach. She's known to her students as Dr. Hoffoss, and to her artist friends, especially in the Burning Man community, as Sparkle.[10] Her first contact with Burning Man left Diane with the distinct sense that what most art professors profess was actually true: *everybody is an artist*. Out of a sense of frustration with American politics, and seeking an outlet for that frustrations, she set out to create and show three pieces. "None of them sold," she told Austin when he conducted the interviews for this section, "but it was the first time I did an art thing."

Having *done an art thing*, Diane started to play around with the possibility of designing a sculpture that highlighted a mathematical puzzle. Knowing this would require her to learn more about how large art was built drew her to a project that provided relevant experience, though it had nothing to do with "mathematical art." It was, however, an opportunity to work on a large and complex installation. Diane's role initially involved translating between the artist, whose broad vision drove the process, and the engineer, whose specific actions realized the piece. But then the engineer moved on to other things, and Diane found herself at the helm of both lighting and software.

Diane's experience mediating between people left her curious about actually making art herself. But what she needed was an idea. It was about that time that Satyan Devadoss joined the university. He was excited to again be teaching an upper division class on discrete and computational geometry. What he loves most about that class, he said when interviewed for this Element, is the use of art to address unsolved mathematics problems.

When Satyan invited Diane to help design a final assignment that matched on this core idea, Diane leapt at the opportunity. Together they challenged their students to propose a concept for a large-scale sculpture with three criteria. The sculpture must (1) respond to that year's Burning Man theme: *I, Robot*; (2) be interactive; and (3) address an unsolved question in geometry. While Diane was keen to produce something that convinced the decision-makers at Burning Man, Satyan was excited to see what students made of the *unsolved question* challenge.

As the homework came in, one proposal stood out. Three undergraduate students had proposed an unfolding dodecahedron. They loved the way the thing unfolded. Diane and Satyan noted that adding mirrors to a dodecahedron might allow them to mimic one of the universe's possible shapes (nobody knows for sure, it turns out). Recent data from NASA's Wilkinson Microwave Anisotrophy Probe had suggested that the universe might indeed be conceptualized using concepts first developed by Poincaré. Diane remembered back to

---

[10] For this section Austin interviewed all four protagonists: Diane Hoffoss, Gordon Hoople, Nate Parde, and Satyan Devadoss.

an undergrad internship working with mathematician Jeff Weeks, which got her thinking about using mirrors to simulate this shape of space (though to this day it remains unclear just who thought of mirrors first). With all the components in place by November, the design was submitted for consideration to the Burning Man Project (see Figures 1 and 2).

To everyone's delight, the piece – the concept of the piece – received partial funding from the San Diego Collaborative Arts Project and was accepted for inclusion at Burning Man the following August. And just as suddenly as it started, the semester was over. It was December and the students headed home for the holidays and went on with their lives.

As the students moved on, and as Satyan's attention turned to funding their initiative, and as the new year dawned, Diane faced the reality: Someone was going to have to figure out how to actually build the thing. Immediately, a dilemma presented itself: The piece was designed to unfold entirely, origami-like. This could be accomplished affordably using canvas and wood – indeed, Diane proposed this as an option in the original proposal. The problem was that wood and canvas are flimsy, and the piece wouldn't have lasted long. The other way to accomplish an origami-like unfolding would be to find high-tech materials that cut weight dramatically. The problem then became the cost of exotic ultralight materials. Nobody could afford those.

Figure 1 Weeks' representation of the Poincaré Dodecahedron. Reprinted with permissions from the American Mathematics Society (Weeks, 2004).

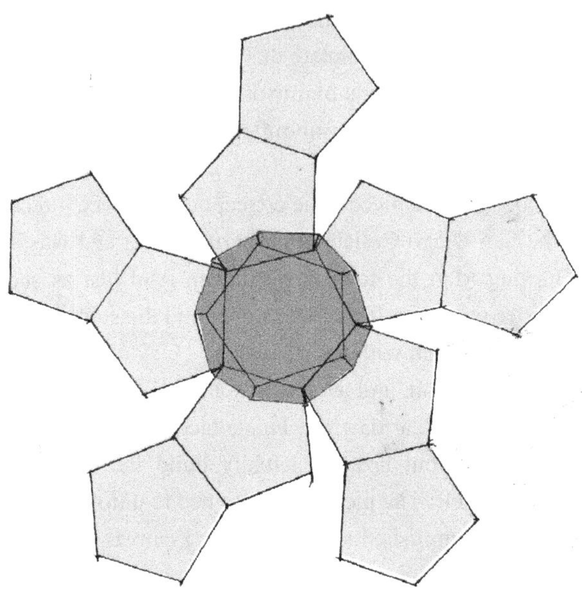

Figure 2 Student representation of unfolding Dodecahedral Space. Photo Credit: Diane Hoffoss.

The key design concept – the unfolding universe echoed by an origami unfolding of the panels – was diametrically opposed to a key cost constraint. The challenge could have been solved with much lighter panels and sophisticated lifting mechanisms, but that all would have added cost. The solution, Diane quickly realized, was going to require more hands and minds. Shifting the piece from concept-stage sketch to the real-build world would require volunteers with expertise in engineering, materials science, and electronic systems.

The piece, in other words, could have been built under the lead artist model, with a single vision alongside a very large budget. The budget could have gone toward hiring people with the requisite technical skills to accomplish the task set out for them by a lead artist, and the requisite socio-emotional skills to work with or around the lead artist. It could have been built this way, and indeed many large pieces are the result of a singular creative self taking credit for an accomplishment that required many other hands and minds.

What actually happened is that a number of people with a variety of skills over a stretch of time worked in different teams – sometimes collaborating and sometimes conflicting – and managed to build a rather large piece of art, within a rather short period of time, with rather a small budget, while also somehow managing to have an experience they wanted to refine and repeat.

Diane's quest for collaborators led her to Gordon, and later our colleague in the Theater Department, Nate Parde, Gordon's training in mechanical engineering made him a perfect match for the technical challenge, and Nate's experience in the fast-pace and solutions-oriented world of theater made him a perfect match for the trial and error efforts needed to take the piece off the drawing board. Others proved crucial as well, including Max, who supported Diane on the electronic side of things, and Quinn, a student whose help was crucial in the initial engineering design of the project.

Over an intensive six-month period stretching from March to August the piece began to take shape. In our university's engineering workshop Gordon led students as they worked to translate concepts and sketches into the final structure. Through long hours on back-to-back days Gordon's team of students slowly made progress on one technical challenge after another. When Gordon told me about this period, I could sense his pride. "We built," he told me, "a really great team."

Meanwhile, in a community art space called CoLab, Diane gathered a growing number of people – more than forty, when it was all said and done – focused on sheathing the structure, connecting all of the electronics, and getting the lighting just right. Weekend after weekend, as growing numbers of people clustered in little groups over particular projects, an *esprit de corps* emerged. When Austin asked Diane about this time, she lit up, telling him with pride and conviction that what they nurtured was a "spectacularly beautiful community," a tiny public.

Diane and Gordon were essentially working as project managers on their respective components of the project and the people they managed differed dramatically. Gordon's engineering students had signed up for a summer research experience, able to be delegated to tasks on an as-needed basis. The CoLab community, by contrast, was entirely volunteer-based. For Diane, the coordination of projects, people, and resources was incredibly stressful. It was impossible to know who would show up to help, what skills they might have, and whether they would come back next time in order to complete a task.

Managing students who are tasked with being on time and coordinating volunteers who don't necessarily have to show up at all led to the emergence of two different leadership styles. Some of the differences were dispositional, since Gordon and Diane are different people, but they faced particular challenges and opportunities that were the result of the people available to support the project.

While Gordon was at the helm of an organized team, and Diane was at the heart of an all-volunteer community, tensions emerged when these two approaches came into contact. In one case that both Diane and Gordon remembered clearly, Gordon's decision to redesign a structural element threw into disarray Diane's design plan, as a new supporting beam now bisected the path of a critical lighting strip.

Regular dialogue between the workshop and the art space teams might have prevented such misunderstandings, but the August installation date was fast approaching for each group. And anyway, there was no overarching coordinating process for anticipating and addressing these challenges. They were discovered at the point of impact, when engineering solution collided with artistic intent. It would not be until much later that Diane and Gordon, joined by Nate and Austin, would create an organizational structure (ArtBuilds) in order to formalize a project-based divisions of labor and invest in community-building.

In late August, the piece was installed at Burning Man, in the Black Rock Desert of Nevada, and in October, it was installed at Balboa Park, in San Diego, California. When all was said and done, more than eighty people had poured 6,500 hours bringing three students' ideas for an unsolved math problem into the world as a physical artifact (Figures 3 and 4).

Figure 3 Installing Unfolding Humanity (2018), Burning Man (Black Rock City, Nevada). Photo Credit: Gordon Hoople.

Figure 4 Diane, Gordon, Nate, and Satyan with Unfolding Humanity (2018), Balboa Park (San Diego, California). Photo Credit: Satyan L Devadoss.

Art as Collective Action

Large-scale art requires lots of people serving in many different roles. There are the people with the original vision, the people who articulate that vision, the people who make that vision a reality, and the people who say what all that means. Mainstream art worlds only have one crown to place on one head – *where's the artist?* they wonder.

Unfolding Humanity could have been built under dramatically different conditions. Satyan could have given the students an A in the class, then hand their drawings over to a series of material and construction experts, who then build the thing, allowing him to stand in front of it and talk about how inspired he was by students, and how he believes art and mathematics have so much they can learn from one another.

That familiar approach fundamentally ignores the effective team Gordon built in the engineering workshop, and the close community Diane developed in the CoLab art space. The traditional account erases the imaginative people. It also erases the iterative process. It disappears the collective intelligence. It neatly tucks the generative capacities of the many hands and minds back beyond a series of contracts and subcontracts. It highlights only the name of the signing artist – the coordinator, the conceptualizer, and communicator bundled into one – as if they are the only one.

This process is not an exception in the world of large-scale art. It is instead a full, frank, and transparent account of the rule. The lead artist duo Christo and Jeanne-Claude funded their ambitious large-scale installations by selling sketches and preparatory works. The actual art was built by others. Realizing the artists' vision for Wrapped Reichstag, 1971–1995 (Berlin), required more than 200 workers, 95 of whom were professional climbers, and none of whom, presumably, could be mistaken for the artist (Christo and Jeanne-Claude, nd).

Big art is a collective accomplishment. Large-scale sculptures often require collective action. Here we would do well to remember that *Unfolding Humanity* did not emerge from an artist collective. It was instead an ad hoc collaboration that formed because the original design could only be instantiated by many people with expertise in multiple areas. And what happens when many people work together? There are challenges. And joys.

Art Practice as Community Building

Diane might not have set out with the intention to build a community of kindred spirits at the CoLab art space, and Gordon might not have set out to build a high-performing team of workers at the engineering workshop, but both came away with a strong sense that they *wanted to do that again*. This determination comes from an appreciation for both process and the final outcome. Both wanted to build art again, and to continue doing it with others, and to do so with clearer lines of communication and divisions of labor. If those are their takeaways, what are the larger lessons for how we think about art as collective action? Austin's sense is that there are three points at which this case is suggestive of much larger trends.

First, each had a different metaphor for the kind of collaboration that *Unfolding Humanity* represented. Diane, who drew inspiration from the "radical inclusion" commitments of Burning Man, described the process of welcoming the flow of new people into CoLab's creative space as "exceptionally beautiful," and led to an "unbelievable, wonderful community" and recalled that someone, in the furious midst of the work, commented to her that "you're not just making an art project, you're making community."

When Austin spoke to Gordon about that period, Gordon reflected on how much work had been invested by his team in the workshop. He explained that the project simply couldn't have happened without the team of students. It was clear that this experience was formative for Gordon's thinking about what makes for a good team.

Nate, for his part, said that the collaborative capacity demonstrated in this process looked a great deal like the collaborative model found in theater. The director is important, but knows better than to tell the lighting designer how to do their job. Certainly there is a playwright, but they are often elsewhere. Or dead.

Satyan, for his part, was adamant that he was looking for collaborations that could help reverse what he considers to be a deeply entrenched imbalance between popular respect for mathematics and the common dismissal of art. He was at pains to emphasize that, in his collaborations with artists, the goal is for art and mathematics to be in dialogue, rather than for a mathematician to dictate what an artist should do. He was much more interested, he told me, in kicking the ball the other way: "I want the art to say something to mathematics," such that mathematicians could learn from artists.

What struck Austin across these conversations is the reference to dramatically different metaphors – community in an art space warehouse, a team in a workshop, individuated experts in a theater, academics on a soccer field. None of these are correct or incorrect, but each point to the numerous forms collaboration can take, and the diverse ways those forms can be conceptualized.

Second, the *artist* identity is complicated. Diane was honest about how frustrating it was to have shepherded the student's design out of the classroom and to be responsible for ensuring it made its way into the world, only to run into logistical challenges and second guessing from the engineering team. Yet her frustration grew from a sense that she wasn't consulted as a peer, rather than that she wasn't the final authority as *the artist.*

In fact, the title and role of *artist* is dynamic. Nate told me "I did not think of myself as an artist. I thought of myself as someone who *helps* artists." Likewise, Gordon said that when they started the process "I was an engineer, not an artist." Diane explains she cares about "being thought of as creative and fun, not about being called an 'artist'."

The reason for this shouldn't be surprising. Singular creative selves, especially those granted MFAs in formal art worlds, guard the title assiduously. As the previous section suggests, this shouldn't be surprising. Perhaps we have blamed too much on ego and should instead focus on the fact that we are all vulnerable, each in our own way, to hostile and impersonal market forces. While this may be the case with working artists, we would note that many critics and academic artists spend time celebrating art as a public good and a font of personal growth and exploration, while simultaneously patrolling the boundaries of its actual use.

Despite such gatekeeping, time and experience have eroded this ambivalence, allowing a nascent identity to emerge. "Now I think about myself as an artist," Gordon said in our interview. Notably, this was because he was the person who submitted the proposal for a subsequent installation, and the paperwork that came back listed him as *the artist* – "so I was like *oh, sure, that's fine.*" Gordon has thought of himself as an artist ever since, though, he notes, "I wouldn't introduce myself to the art faculty as an artist."

Nate, for his part, reflected that there *was* a brief moment, in college, when he thought *maybe I will be an artist.* The moment lasted until his professor noted about his work "this is pretty good work, *for you.*" Austin has a degree in photography but doesn't identify as an artist. Diane, for her part, is still wrestling with the concept, telling Austin in an interview "I think even now, if you said *are you an artist*, I would feel weird. But I feel less weird . . . but I just got offered an art grant . . . so maybe I'm starting to change that vision of myself." Satyan was adamant on this point: He does not identify as an artist and believes a mathematician's claiming of the title to be a form of overreach, considering the status imbalances he considers to already be in play between mathematics and the fine arts.

Brief Epilogue

In the final analysis, *Unfolding Humanity*'s journey into the world offers an x-ray of a process developed to build large-scale art in the traditional art world. The only difference is that we are transparent about the process. The conceptual terrain was laid down by some big thinkers (the professors), a spark of imagination and creativity came from others (students), the design came from a person (Diane), the structure and design leads (Gordon and Diane) had to hash things out bilaterally while also building community and teams, and it took 6,500 hours of eighty people's lives to make the idea real.

This is quite similar to the process described in the previous section and used by Kapoor. Similar, but not identical. The significant difference is that Kapoor is keen on being the lead artist. His name is placed on the gallery placards. Our motives, incentives, and identities are quite different. We got our start building large art for maverick art spaces like Burning Man, where there is no placard, no signature, no opening ceremony, and the piece just might burn.

In the final analysis, this collaboration lasted one full year: from a class in a fall semester, through an intense build phase over winter, spring, and summer, with an installation at Burning Man in late summer to a final installation at the Old Globe Theater in San Diego's Balboa Park in October. After *Unfolding Humanity's* final installation that October, the piece retired into storage for five years. While *Unfolding Humanity* went into storage, the collaborative experience raised questions about what was next for the people who had built it.

ArtBuilds: From Collaboration to Collective (2019–2024)

With *Unfolding Humanity* in the rearview mirror, both Gordon and Diane interpreted the collaboration's challenges as a chance to refine their process, rather than a reason to part ways. And in the path ahead, opportunities could be seen. Diane was motivated by a desire to continue building community and refine artistic details, Gordon was motivated to continue building teams and refine the production process, Nate saw a welcoming space for his imagination and an opportunity to contribute art to a community he loved, and Austin had fallen in love with the people, and was keen to use art to explore themes in his research on politics, culture, and technology.

With these various motivations, the group set to work discussing what they might do next, and the following five years were spent investing in the team (especially with respect to recruitment, retention, communication, and divisions of labor), improving process (especially working out a project workflow that supported work on multiple simultaneous projects), developing artistic capacity (especially increasing the quality of our work and diversifying who could do what), and formalizing organization (especially by starting a nonprofit and facilitating regular events).

In Year 2, the group returned to Burning Man with a fresh piece of art. Discussions over drinks had led to the construction of a giant sundial. Gordon and Austin's work on the original design was completely upended by an offhand suggestion from Nate that quickly turned into a group effort, as Nate weighed in with experience constructing sets for theater, and Diane came alongside to contribute to programming the LEDs that lit the piece and, perhaps more important, found the volunteers that made it possible to successfully burn the piece. Austin loved the possibility that time just does what it does – not much we can do about time – but that interchangeable discs on the sides of the sculpture suggested that we may enter a world defined by structures and institutions, but what we make of them is up to us (an early homage to the pragmatic philosophy of Roberto Mangabeira Unger; see

Figure 5 About Time (2019) at Burning Man, Side Profile (Black Rock City, Nevada). Photo Credit: Gordon Hoople.

Figures 5 and 6). Participants could climb inside and create their own message to the outside world. We were supremely pleased that the piece burned exactly the way we had planned (Figure 7 and via YouTube).

As a global pandemic shut the world down, the team pivoted to virtual spaces, sharing design ideas in the online platform Miro, and buying just-released VR headset from Oculus to design and iterate in virtual space. If online spaces helped the group think about design, the larger set of puzzles emerged from the real world. Political tensions were on the rise, the media landscape was permeated with distrust, and a global lockdown left people wondering if there was a light at the end of the ever-constricting tunnel. These themes began to show up in the group's work.

The concepts of constriction and emergence found their way into a challenge we tasked to Gordon's engineering students. The constraint was simple: come up with ideas that can be built of easy-to-transport materials, in particular wood. The design that ultimately caught our eyes was a huge caterpillar (Figure 8). We

Figure 6 About Time (2019) at Burning Man, Interior (Black Rock City, Nevada). Photo Credit: Austin Choi-Fitzpatrick.

Figure 7 About Time (2019) at Burning Man, Burning (Black Rock City, Nevada). Photo Credit: Austin Choi-Fitzpatrick.

Figure 8 Original concept from engineering students (2021). Photo Credit: Austin Choi-Fitzpatrick.

took that back to our team – now clearly comprised of Gordon, Nate, Austin, and Diane – and in that process the notion of constraint and expansion became clear, and we tasked students with determining the feasibility of the piece. A prototype, aptly titled *Emergence*, was installed in the Mojave Desert at an art event called Everywhen (Figure 9). It was Year 3 of our project (2021), as humanity slowly emerged from the pandemic.

The world might have been exiting lockdown, but the United States, *where* we live, was entering a political crisis. The role of lenses and filters in shaping *what* we see – a direct nod to the way a distorted media landscape affects how we see the world—found its way into a project called *Reflexion*, funded by the City of San Diego. Commissioned mid-pandemic, the piece was one of many sponsored with an eye toward getting people back to city parks once the pandemic ended. We were pleased that our concept was chosen for installation

Figure 9 Emergence (2021) at Everywhen (Mojave Desert, California). Photo Credit: Annastasia Rose Beal.

in the iconic Ellen Browning Scripps Park, and we did our best to finalize a site-specific piece that reflected the location's beauty (Figure 10).

At the same time we were building *Reflexion*, the team was working on a much larger-scale version of *Emergence*. The construction (Gordon and Nate) and lighting (Diane) sides of the design discussions also saw an opportunity to increase the scale and electronic complexity of the piece. *Re:Emergence* made its way to Burning Man in Year 4 of our Collective. The concept, that humanity had passed through an incredibly tight space, was joined by a growing sense – for Austin especially, drawing on Karl Marx and (again) on Roberto Unger – that *we make history, but not under conditions of our own choosing.* We have the ability to act and shape the world we find ourselves in. Two simple-seeming axioms are baked into this argument: (1) We can shape the world; but (2) we cannot choose which world we land in. That's Marx. And Unger, for his part, pushes us to recognize that everything we see that is solid (institutions, norms,

Figure 10 Reflexion (2021), Ellen Browning Scripps Park (La Jolla, California). Photo Credit: Frank Guthrie.

etc.) is the product of human agency. They exist because people decided to act, individually, collectively, civilizationally, and for better or for worse.

This isn't necessarily *why* we built *Re:Emergence*, but it is how Austin described the way the piece spoke to the current moment. The outside of the structure gained symbolic meaning (again, perhaps only for Austin) as it spatially represented the idea that we can perhaps *climb outside of and exit entirely the tight spaces life places us in*. Again, the interplay of structure and agency emerges as a key aspect of ArtBuilds narrative but remains separate from the acts of conceptualization and construction (Figure 11).

The process of designing, constructing, and installing these pieces from Years 2–4 involved regular meetings (via Zoom during the Pandemic, and later in Nate's back patio), welcoming new people into the team, wishing well those who moved on to other things, building a website, clarifying roles, and registering as a nonprofit.

By the time we came back from our Year 4 installation of *Re:Emergence* at Burning Man it was clear that we had what it took to make our art better. And by "have what it takes" we mean that we had built the people and community that Diane had so aspired to in the community art space she cultivated at Colab all

Figure 11 Re:Emergence (2022), Burning Man (Black Rock City, Nevada). Photo Credit: Frank Guthrie.

those years ago, but that we had also developed the capacity and process that Gordon aspired to build with his workshop-based team. ArtBuilds was both a team *and* a community.

In Year 5, it was this team and community that was awarded Honorarium funding from the Burning Man Project to reprise Unfolding Humanity. The money would go toward refining structural elements, overhauling electronics, and simplifying the interactivity. Over the course of six months a clear and coherent team made its way through the project in a single space: Nate's theater, where all teams worked together in real time (Figure 12). In the fall of Year 5, the piece returned to Burning Man (Figure 13). Reflecting on how far the group has come in the past five years Gordon mused that "I would be fine if we had zero new people and focused exclusively on refining our team."

Conclusion

Our story of how a class becomes a collaboration, and how a collaboration becomes a collective allows us to see three things. First, our collaboration benefited immensely from a critical, but often overlooked, factor: The key protagonists in this story – Nate, Diane, Gordon, Satyan, and Austin – are all tenured faculty members at a relatively well-resourced university. We are extremely privileged to have something like parity in terms of our baseline resources, our capacity to share our time, our need for compensation, and our desire for recognition.

Power imbalances, unless properly managed, can destabilize collective efforts. We can imagine hurdles along these lines. Perhaps one does not have the financial resources to volunteer for a nonprofit and to spend money going to art events. Perhaps one does not have the time to commit, since all free time is

Figure 12 Unfolding Humanity (2023) Under Construction in USD's Studio Theater. Photo Credit: Frank Guthrie.

Figure 13 Unfolding Humanity (2023), Burning Man (Black Rock City, Nevada). Photo Credit: Duncan Rawlinson.

directed toward uncompensated solidarity and training efforts (as happens to many colleagues with minoritized identities). Perhaps one struggles to have their voice heard, and as a result final decisions are less collective than they would otherwise be. Perhaps there is a clear status difference between "leadership" and everyone else. Not addressing these issues prevents the emergence of the very inclusive and equitable collaborative environments we set out to nurture.

Second, we note an inflection point, after the original *Unfolding Humanity* installation was complete, when the collaboration could have ended *or* a lead artist could have emerged *or* a collective could have formed. Our assessment is that the emergence of a collective was the result of Diane's commitment to community-building combined with Gordon's commitment to project management.

Third, this overview helps us to get a feel for how important it was that Diane decided to take action, rather than sitting on her hands during a political crisis, and how important it was that Satyan set aside time for his students to play around with an idea, and how important it was that Gordon and Diane invested in building coherent teams. None of this, of course, was on our minds in the midst of it all, but our experience led us into conversations with others who are experimenting in this same collaborative maverick art space.

We did not set out to become a maverick artist collective. As it turns out, opportunities for collaboration abound, but you need the right conditions. Pursuing those opportunities results in play, solidarity, creative freedom, and new ideas. Cultivating these opportunities requires cheap space, institutional resources, and supportive norms. Those ideas occupy the remainder of this Element.

4 The Landscape: Elements of Connective Creativity

Our experience with ArtBuilds is just that, *ours*. Over the years we have developed hunches about how connective creativity works. But are we right? In an effort to find out we set out to interview others working in this space. Gordon led a series of interviews with artists working in collectives and collaborations, asking them about their experiences (see the Methods Appendix for details). These data, along with our combined decade of participant observation in ArtBuilds and Burning Man, revealed three key aspects of connective creativity: building a collective identity, making time for play, and leveraging resources. In this section, we take a deeper dive into each of these ideas.

Build a Shared Identity

When it comes to collaboration, the whole is greater than the sum of its parts. In his interviews, Gordon heard this refrain time and time again. The work that comes from collaborations is so much more than the individual pieces that each of the artists contributed. People often describe the situation as magical. While everyone has their own unique skills, it is nearly impossible to define who contributed what to a truly collaborative piece art. It's the process of *working together* that created the emergent ideas that eventually manifested as a new piece of art. When we shared the early draft of this manuscript with Diane, she responded to the line "truly impossible to define who contributed what" with this:

> I love this! This is so true, even in parts I know I was involved with. For example, I can't remember whether it was me or Lee who thought of the mirrors, but I know it arose while we were spitballing about how to do the humanity part of the sculpture. Satyan was there too at that conversation, so it's also possible he said the word *mirror* first. So not only is it hard for me to say what generated that idea, it's even hard for me to remember who said the word first.

What makes this magic happen? A critical element seems to be the creation of a *shared identity*. Artists stop thinking of the piece as "mine" and start thinking of it as "ours." This was perhaps best exemplified in Gordon's conversation with *3B Collective*. On their website they describe themselves as a "collective of Indigenous, African American and Chicano artists and designers that produce original works along with helping artists, institutions, and galleries we respect with large-scale, site-specific installations and murals."[11] Their projects all focus on social justice, a central theme in their shared identity.

The group formed during their studies at UCLA. As Oscar Magallanes recalled "The thing that really brought us together. I think a lot of it actually has to do with systemic racism. I mean, there's very few people who have our backgrounds in these art programs and so we kind of gravitated towards each other." We saw this same pattern in all of the artists we spoke with – there was a central connection that brought the group together: *To Do Mending Project* was united by the need to do *something* after the divisive election of Donald Trump, *Las Hermanas Iglesias* were united by both sisterhood and parallel journeys through challenging MFA programs, and our own collective *ArtBuilds* was brought together by an interest in the maverick art space of Burning Man.

---

[11] 3B Collective. "Who We Are." Accessed February 14, 2024. https://3bcollective.com/.

As Oscar explained the origins of *3B Collective* further, he realized "We call it our collective, but it's also a bit of a support group, I think, which we don't talk about a lot." His comment stuck with Gordon, who realized that he felt exactly the same way about our own collective. Sure, we make art together, but we are also there for each other when things go sideways – art related or otherwise. For all of the artists groups we spoke with this seemed to ring true, their collaboration wasn't just a professional activity that happened during the 9 to 5 working day. The relationship and support component was a central element of why folks worked well together. Folks weren't friendly in a professional sense, they really seemed to know one other. They had built the trust necessary for people to let down their guard. And once people let down their guard, they are more likely to try things out, to share, and to play. For *3B Collective*, building a shared identity was instrumental in battling the barriers put in place by systemic racism. As Oscar explains:

> For me, it stuck out that [Chicano artists] were able to circumvent a lot of these barriers by working collaboratively. And over the years, I had seen it, where they were coming together, to pool the resources and to do jobs that they couldn't do on their own . . . . And that's kind of the way we approach things, to try to battle this hyper-individualistic way of really, like, artists become this brand . . . . So, we just wanted to make it very clear that we are working together, we're working collaboratively, [and] we're addressing issues of systemic racism.

For all of these artists we spoke with, the creation of a strong shared identity is predicated on cultivating a deep sense of psychological safety. Psychological safety describes a person's perception of the consequences of taking interpersonal risks. When we feel comfortable with a group, we are more willing to voice our ideas, disagree with someone, or step up to a challenge. The literature suggests that psychological safety is a key element for supporting creativity in teams (Edmondson, 1999).

So, what happens when we build this collective identity? Everyone we spoke with emphasized that the art that came out of collaborations had an emergent property – it was not something that came from a single person's mind. As Brian, of artist team *Brian & Ryan*, explains:

> It's not just Brian brings his part and Ryan brings his part. There is this new creature that is born, that it's its own thing, its own aesthetic. And there may be pieces that we've brought into it. There may be pieces that we take out of it, but there's something unique about that moment where we've created something together. That in my mind really would not have existed without that collaboration. It wasn't like I do half the canvas; you do half the canvas. It's like, well, let's rethink the canvas.

Many of the artists we interviewed had been formally trained, receiving MFAs from prestigious programs. A constant theme we heard from them, as well as artists without formal training, was the upskilling involved in establishing their own unique voice, something to differentiate themselves as artists. They spoke of learning how to create a coherent body of work in conversation with itself – following a particular set of themes that made sense to mainstream art worlds, and the market forces they would need to adapt to in order to support themselves. As one artist said of their MFA program: "You learn a lot about that individualistic stuff, and you kind of get it shoved down your throat."

In the very next breath, we'd hear about how collaboration offered a chance to create identities outside of this tightly controlled space. Sisters Janelle and Lisa Iglesias, of *Las Hermanas Iglesias*, described to Gordon how they both came to artmaking separately, each taking their own journey, but somehow along parallel tracks. Fortuitously, they ended up enrolled in MFA programs in different cities at the same point in time. Long before the days of Zoom and screen sharing, the Iglesias sisters' artistic collaboration relied on an ancient technology: the US Postal Service. Their collaboration was stitched together package by package as they mailed artifacts back and forth during graduate school. As Janelle said of the early stages of this collaboration:

> There was a kind of sense of freedom that [our projects together] didn't have to be within a conversation or trajectory of one's work. That was this tight knit narrative of what this person makes. It could be this very experiential place where we decided that the whole purpose was sort of, to explore a sense of freedom and to break our own rules and come up with new ones. And that it was this very kind of productive, creative place, and that there was a sort of protected sense of working together that maybe we could do things together that we might feel self-conscious or vulnerable, doing separately.

By constructing a fresh and collective identity that was distinct from their individual practices, it was suddenly possible for Janelle and Lisa to take on all kinds of ambitious and experimental projects. In our interviews we heard stories about artists working in genres outside of their defined lane (e.g., painters collaborating on performance art) and others spoke of violating unwritten rules (e.g., using an iPhone to shoot photography). In our own collective, we have seen how a shared identity can create even more radical changes – allowing, for example, engineers, mathematicians, or sociologists to try their hand at art, crossing the heavily policed disciplinary boundaries of the academy. These collective identities give artists – or really anyone with a creative spark – the freedom to deviate from expectations.

Indeed, a major benefit of building a collective identity is that it empowers the individuals in the group to grow. For example, Gordon heard from many of the (non-white male) artists he spoke with about their hesitation to adopt the title of artist. As Sheena Dowling of *Collective Memory* explains:

> Unlearning of this idealized, romanticized concept of the artist and personally really acknowledging this truth that I believe that we all are artists, and we all are creative people, and we can take ownership of that identity whenever we decide . . . it's been important because it's something I struggled with where I felt like I wasn't a real artist, but I really wanted to be.

For many interviewees, the creation of a collective identity helped them to break free of the pressures usually experienced by solo artists. A collective identity allows solo artists to play with genre, medium, voice, and tone. The cooperative act pulls a scrim across what is essentially a creative research and development sandbox, freeing the individual to experiment.

Building a collective identity is critical to supporting connective creativity. The transition from *mine* to *ours,* and from *I* to *we,* and from *me* to *us* represents not only a lowering of the ego and an increase in trust but also the creation of a shared sense of identity that allows for the emergence of what some experts refer to as an idioculture, that is, a shared system of ideas, norms, and behaviors that is shared by members of a small group (Fine, 1979: 734). The net effect is deeper trust, faster communication, clearer roles, and better tools for resolving breakdowns in trust, communication, and roles. All that boring stuff serves as background conditions for learning to go with the flow.

Make Time for Play

We have argued that collective identity can be a product of cooperation. We have also argued that a shared identity as a cooperative might allow individual artists the time, space, and freedom to let their professional guard down. Perhaps the ego and commerce rules of the integrated and mainstream art world are suspended for a moment if one can just take a deep breath, remember why they got into this in the first place, and just have fun. We are writing from within the status game of academia, where perverse incentive structures reduce the likelihood that we play outside our sub-disciplinary niches. Art worlds have their own norms around exactly how much stylistic variation can fit within one individual brand identity.

Play, then, is a kind of joy-ridden and whole-hearted experimentation with the possible. Childhood is perhaps the last time many of us played, so absorbed in an activity that we lose track of time, entering what Hungarian-American psychologist Mihaly Csikszentmihalyi (1990) refers to as a state of flow. We should seek these opportunities out. In her bestselling *The Artist's Way* (2022: 18) Julia

Cameron recommends inviting these moments. An Artist Date, she argues, is a crucial window of time:

> especially set aside and committed to nurturing your creative consciousness, your inner artist. In its most primary form, the Artist Date is an excursion, a play date that you preplan and defend against all interlopers. You do not take anyone on this Artist Date but you and your inner artist, a.k.a. your creative child.

This is good advice, and our interviews suggest it is doubly true when *playing with others*. In fact, play was central to collaboration in almost every group we interviewed. When Gordon spoke with artist Arzu Ozkal, one of the very first things she told him was *"I like to play. I don't have time to get bored. I don't like to take myself too seriously as an artist. I just like to get messy."* As their conversation continued, the theme of play returned again and again. Arzu emphasized how important it was to have collaborators that one can trust to play with. Creativity requires someone to bounce bad ideas off of, without judgment. Playful and low-cost experimentation can lead to new ideas.

Artist duo *Brian & Ryan* shared this sentiment. They have been working together for two decades and quite literally began their collaboration with play. Their first works together involved a series of absurdist competitions. For example, in one piece they attached basketball hoops to their backs and played against each other in front of an audience. During our interview they emphasized they really were *playing* these competitions – they would create the ground rules, but the rest wasn't scripted – it was pure play. Reflecting on their work together, Ryan realized:

> [The collaborative] *Brian & Ryan* occupies this space that allows us to play out ideas that we wouldn't play out in our own practices . . . I think it allows us to kind of spread our ideas a little bit in this playground, right, a kind of safe play space. . . . if you're afraid that the person you're talking to . . . might actually judge you or might actually shoot your idea down . . . then you're less likely to come up with a really interesting idea, because people are withholding. Brian and I are comfortable enough. I mean, our collaboration goes from studio to workshop, to the kitchen table . . . We're willing to say things out loud to one another that we wouldn't say to anybody else. And we've drawn things on paper. We're like this is hilarious. Burn it. This can never be shown. Never let it out.

This is a truly remarkable kind of play. Brian and Ryan, through their collective identity as *Brian & Ryan*, have created a conceptual playground – one where they can come together without fear of reprisals. Their relationship is deep, allowing them to share boundary-pushing ideas that they wouldn't otherwise share.

It is this freedom to play that so many artists emphasized in our conversations. They wanted to work together because it was a chance to do something fun, learn from a friend, come up with new ideas, get outside their head, and perhaps even outside their genre. In conversation after conversation we heard others say what we ourselves know to be true: play and playfulness grease the wheels of the creative process – creating a safe environment with trusted confidants to explore new ideas together.

Bias For Action

One of ArtBuilds' core values is a bias for action. Our general approach to getting started is not to come up with a plan, but to instead start tinkering. Satyan and Diane, working with their students, might come up with a clever concept for an art piece (*Unfolding Humanity*), but have absolutely no idea how to build it. Diane keeps going with the idea anyway, confident that she can find the people to help her turn the vision into a reality. Slowly, one by one, people join the project, filing critical gaps that we didn't even know existed. In our own practice we are constantly finding ourselves at the end of a project grateful for all those people who stepped in to make things happen. But none of those people would have come alongside if we had waited for everything to be in place before we started creating.

In the highly regarded *Art & Fear: Observations on the Perils (and Rewards) of Artmaking*, artists and authors David Bayles and Ted Orland (2001: 9) explore the psychological challenges faced by artists. Their advice resonates with our experience. As they summarize, "Basically, those who continue to make art are those who have learned how to continue – or more precisely, have learned how to not quit." Making art is an incredibly hard and scary prospect. It turns out that the ability to keep making art despite this terror is what sets successful artists apart. Along the same vein, brothers Tom and David Kelley, founders of IDEO and the Stanford d.School, emphasize the importance of just getting started. In *Creative Confidence: Unleashing the Creative Potential Within Us All* (2013), they explain their now-ubiquitous approach to design thinking. A key tenet of design thinking is to embrace imperfection and start making, even with incomplete information. It is through prototyping that people learn what it is they are really trying to make, what is and is not working, and where they should go next. Our interviews revealed that this bias for action is a key and consistent phenomenon in artistic collaborations. In reflecting on the genesis of *Collective Memory*, artist Rae Dowling noted:

> We have to do something about the pandemic and processing the trauma that's come up for people. . . . That's the endpoint. Let's figure out all the stuff in between.

Collaborative artists seem to recognize that once the kernel of an idea is there, the details will get worked out. What's important is to take action – to start working on the sculpture, performance, or experience – and trust that the collaboration path unfolds before us.

The *To Do Mending Project* emerged out of a shared feeling that the world needed mending after the divisive 2016 elections. Founders Michelle Montjoy, Anna O'Cain, and Siobhán Arnold wanted to create experiences that empowered people to come together to repair things in community, sitting around a table and talking while they worked. Rather than fully program the project, the team just started doing it. They found someone willing to let them use a gallery space for the project. They invited their friends to help by hosting workshops – ranging from how to make pasta to how to glue things together. And then they opened the doors and started mending. It all came together.

What we heard time and again from artists is that their projects never quite ended up the way they imagined. It was in the doing that they discovered what actually needed to be done. (This Element, as it happens, came together exactly the same way. We didn't figure out what it was about until we were nearly finished writing.) Having a bias for action seems to be both a necessary precondition and a best practice for connective creativity, much as it is in collective action for other forms of social engagement, like social movements and protest politics. In working with others, collaborative artists have to be willing to try things, even when we have no idea what we are doing. The artists we spoke with were comfortable with this ambiguity.

A bias for action appears to be a crucial catalyst for connective creativity. It allows for an organic development of ideas, as the doing itself often reveals unforeseen possibilities. Embracing the unknown and trusting in the collaborative process increases both risks and rewards. This aligns with the concept of "bricolage," where artists utilize existing resources and embrace improvisation to create something unique and powerful.

Furthermore, the willingness to start creating without a predefined plan fosters a sense of shared ownership and responsibility among collaborators. Each individual contributes their own skills and perspectives. This collaborative spirit fosters an environment of learning and growth, where artists can experiment, take risks, and push their creative boundaries. Ultimately, this bias for action acts as a driving force behind the collaborative process, enabling artists to achieve remarkable results that exceed their initial expectations.

Conclusion

While we have explored the importance of a shared identity, making time for play, and fostering a bias for action as separate threads, these elements are the warp and weft of successful artistic collaborations. From the shared purpose and goals that forge a strong collective identity, collaborators embark on playful explorations, not only discovering groundbreaking ideas without fear of failure but also strengthening their bonds with each other, nurturing trust and camaraderie.

Trust and camaraderie, in turn, reinforce a bias for action, where individuals willingly jump in and cocreate, even when the path forward is shrouded in uncertainty. This collective energy surpasses individual limitations, not only manifesting as new artistic achievements but also cultivating a vibrant and dynamic ecosystem for creativity to flourish.

5 The Path Ahead: Promoting Connective Creativity

We are building art in uncertain times. The world is witnessing a resurgence in violent conflict, the onset of a climate catastrophe, and we're all bracing for the full impact of artificial intelligences. Tectonic changes are coming in geopolitics, energy, science, and technology that are likely to increase challenges related to poverty, migration, inequality, conflict, and planetary habitability (Choi-Fitzpatrick, 2024). The world has a long list of needs: better politicians, better systems, more trust and civility, better tools for debating, fewer people willing to go along with the status quo, and so forth.

We would like to add to that list a need for creative and positive visions for the future. More time should be tithed to imagining what we want to build and create together, as opposed to how badly everything could go wrong. The concept of *loss aversion* suggests humans are more psychologically and emotionally engaged with the project of avoiding loss than pursuing opportunity (Kahneman, 2011). Humans are better at imagining what can go wrong than dreaming of how to set things right. To make things worse, paths to decisive action are snarled by complex trade-offs, in which no clearly good choice is readily available. Austin has used the notion of *wicked problems* to refer to those moments in which all possible decisions involve undesirable trade-offs (Choi-Fitzpatrick, Irvin-Erickson, and Verdeja, 2022).

It is at the end of this Element that we can now ask the question *why build big art with other people*? Whyever do that, and why do it now, in such challenging times? We wrote this Element because we believe fast times require us to slow down. Changing times require discernment. The arts represent an important space humans have carved out for experimentation and discovery. As a student of social change, Austin is convinced that humanity's stockpile of Utopias has grown dangerously low. We are in desperate need of new ideas and we are in desperate need of community. Why build big art with others? Because uncertain times require both community and creativity.

Community

On the face of it, our art practice makes no sense. We bring huge, heavy, expensive sculptures to an inhospitable desert in the middle of nowhere. Getting the installation ready requires an intensive sprint over the summer months, with dozens of people working together over every spare hour of the day, often on boring and repetitive tasks. When assembling our sculptures we routinely experience 50 MPH winds that drive dust clouds so severe we can't see our feet. To top it all off, sometimes the art exists for just a week before we burn it to the ground. One of our official t-shirts has the Programmers Credo on the back: *We do this not because it is easy, but because we thought it would be easy.* Despite all this, people come back year after year to make art with us. And they invite their friends.

So why do people join us? As near as we can tell, people are motivated by the people they meet, the memories they make, and the friendships they form accomplishing something hard together. In short, people join our projects because they offer the chance to be creative in community. We often hear from new members about how excited they are to have finally found "their people."

Humankind evolved over millennia to exist in tight-knit social groups, but our hyper-connected life is unraveling our communal existence. The trend toward social isolation was most prominently identified by Robert Putman a quarter century ago in *Bowling Alone* (2000). Putman's argument was that American society has long been defined by our memberships in associations that put people into contact with folks who are different than them. As member-ship in groups like the Kiwanis and Rotary Clubs, the YMCA, and even bowling leagues decline, the social fabric becomes more threadbare, and we are lonelier than ever. Writing in the late 1990s Putman was concerned that Americans had too few public places for old friends to gather and too few opportunities to meet new people from different backgrounds.

Things have not gotten better since Putnam put forward this hypothesis. *Bowling Alone* was published a scant three years before Friendster and MySpace launched (in 2003), quickly followed by Facebook in 2004. It is important to remember that for a few years it seemed that the internet really could bring people together and foster vibrant online communities.

Books with titles like *Here Comes Everybody: The Power of Organizing Without Organizations* (Shirkey, 2008) highlighted the potential these platforms had for creating solidarity and civic engagement. As it turns out, social media platforms are powerful tools for creating connections of all sorts, including antidemocratic and race-based solidarities that tear at the social fabric. What's more, at the macro level, platforms like Facebook and X (neé Twitter) brought groups of people together in such a way that exacerbated conflict in the body politic more generally. Once social media companies landed on the advertising business model, surveillance capitalism (Zuboff, 2018) has fatally corrupted what might otherwise have been a powerful platform for lowering the costs of collective action by the powerless (as Shirkey argued in *Here Comes Everybody*) and increasing levels of accountability for the powerful (as Austin argued about democratizing surveillance in Choi-Fitzpatrick, 2020).

The political scientist and historian Benedict Anderson famously argued, in a little book called *Imagined Communities* (1983), that nations are socially constructed communities. The most important part of a collective identity, Anderson determined, was whether or not one perceived themselves to belong to a group that has a particular identity. What would it take to gather more communities of practice around the shared activity of imagining and creating together?

When we are honest with ourselves in this way, the stakes become clearer. Silicon Valley *cannot* be the only place humans do their bravest thinking. We need to foster liberatory imaginations and connective creativity for the public good, for social belonging, for human development, for ecological flourishing. Perhaps we should all be replacing our digital devices for pocket-sized watercolor sets and inviting people to start a band together – even if we don't yet know how to draw or paint or pluck a guitar string.

Creativity

We wrote this Element because we believe dramatically new tools are needed in order to turn the corner with our core commitments (and our capacity to follow through on them) intact. We're thinking of core commitments like those enshrined in the Universal Declaration of Human Rights, and captured more generally in the generous conception of human flourishing we see in the work of Martha Nussbaum (1998, 2006) and the commitment to *making kin* envisioned by Donna Haraway (2016).

Maverick democratic and freespace art worlds, then, for us, are *one place among many* for something very important to take place. What's at stake here, we want to be clear, is not "more democratic and participatory" art at Burning Man (or wherever). Humanity's shared goal should be to fundamentally invest in human creativity – and to do so in a way that builds commitment to serving interplanetary and interspecies flourishing.

We've been thinking about this because, despite how much creativity seems to flourish around us, we can't shake the feeling that society is at risk of having our imaginations and lifeworlds colonized by DARPA and the tech-bros. We're afraid the ocean of the imaginable will be narrowed to a trickle of the profitable.

This would be unfortunate, as creativity is humanity's birthright. We agree with Roberto Unger: what's in us is always more than is in the world. More than in the market. More than in the government. Institutions themselves, in this light, "are desiccated human agency. They are testimony to the last round of collective action, ossified into codes and norms and rules and laws and institutional forms. If we don't like them, then we should change them. But we cannot change things if we cannot imagine for ourselves and create alongside others.

We must limber up for the epoch-defining task of *collectively imagining and co-creating a more just and verdant future for ourselves, and for all others.* We need emancipatory visions for more organic, open-source, and free-range approaches to nurturing imagination and creativity. Otherwise, our emancipatory horizons will be sketched by captains of industry and their technologists, with human society left to the lesser task of coloring inside preset lines. Otherwise, we will only have at hand tools built by people possessing a skewed view of the market, a limited understanding of society, and a complete indifference to flourishing. To life.

This certainly isn't to say that creativity is lacking in places like DARPA, Meta, OpenAI, X, or any of the other alphabet soup characters who have shaped the world we inhabit. Creativity abounds! But it is creativity throttled by the twin grasp of bureaucracy and capitalism, bounded as they are by their own logics, means, and ends. We must be honest with ourselves, when looking at the vast creativity that comes from this sector, that these are too often the pied pipers who call the tune.

When we are honest with ourselves in this way, the stakes become clearer. Silicon Valley *cannot* be the only place humans do their bravest thinking. We need new spaces, new norms, and new institutions built to foster liberatory imaginations and connective creativity for the public good, for human development, for ecological flourishing. Element author Geoff Mulgan (2023) is right: The arts are not prophetic. Rather, they are echolocative, discursive, probing, exploratory, and possibility-expanding. The arts show, not tell.

Supporting Connective Creativity

So how can we increase opportunities for connective creativity? Society, to say nothing of mainstream art worlds, is stuck in a century-long rut. The lone artist model is the default setting for too many art worlds. Yet our conversations with artist collectives and collaborations illuminate the role of play and playfulness, a shared sense of identity, and bias for action. Overall, we were struck by the sheer bootstrappers, if we can coin a term, of it all. Each group, like ours, made things up as they went along. The conditions for connective creativity had to be cobbled together. We must build an ecosystem that fosters cooperation and community. Such an ecosystem requires investments in new ideas and values, new physical and digital spaces, and fresh institutional forms and vision. Importantly, these ideas are not just narrowly applicable to art worlds, but apply more broadly to anyone interested in pursuing collaborative creativity.

Create New Spaces

In *The Death of the Artist* (2020), a book dedicated to cataloging the slings and arrows artists must now survive, author William Deresiewicz convincingly argues that creativity owes a lot to cheap rent in underplanned space, where people can gather to connect and create. Empty space might look like a problem for investors and tax collectors, but they are a key ingredient for fostering creativity. And that empty space is unlikely to be an affordable farmhouse, far from everyone – "Art is a face-to-face business, a matter of intense collaboration and mutual exchange," Deresiewicz (2020: 90) argues, echoing the argument made by sociologist Richard Florida almost two decades previously: "artists move to centers for the same reason coders move to Silicon Valley, because that's where their industries are."

Yet public space for the public good has been consistently eroded over the course of the last three decades. Gentrification has absorbed artists' lofts, economic upturns have overhauled mixed use and abandoned warehouse spaces, and private property claims have constrained the public space available in cities. This decline in communal areas makes connecting hard, whether it is for collective action protests in the streets or collective art construction in a low-rent warehouse space. The impact is felt in the arts, but in politics as well, as public protest – an important research and development zone for democracy – has been cordoned off into ever-narrower "free speech zones."

This isn't to say we lack new places to do new things. Coworking spaces are touted for their potential to foster entrepreneurial collaboration, and innovation zones replete with 3D printers are growing in popularity. But these spaces are in private hands, intended for private use, and often for private gain. Corporations offer many places to connect, for work or play. Yet these often come at a cost – either as an actual financial charge or as the private sector's control over how space gets used.

Meanwhile, public spaces, and places where people can mingle across large differences, are dwindling (Massenkoff and Wilmers, 2023). Our notion of public space is rather broad, encompassing both city parks and sidewalks as well as abandoned lots and empty warehouses. Urban renewal, gentrification, and the encroachment of commerce into every nook and cranny of the public sphere have, especially in America, dramatically reduced the space available for connective creativity and collective action (Choi-Fitzpatrick, 2020: 53).

As private capital expands, the right to the city is in abeyance (Harvey, 2015; Stavrides, 2016), and as civicness recedes from a high-water mark, "free" spaces are harder to find. These spaces include waystations for artists, where rent is cheap and inspiration is plentiful, especially in mountains and deserts, but occasionally still in urban environs. We are thinking of places like Freetown Christiania in Copenhagen, Denmark, Marfa, in Texas, and Bombay Beach at the edge of the Salton Sea here in Southern California.

In many ways, Burning Man is a *temporary autonomous zone*, to borrow a term from the anarchist author Hakim Bey (2003). The temporary and indeed fleeting nature of such autonomous zones is a particularly recent development. Anthropologist David Graeber and archeologist David Wengrow (2021) have argued that much of the ancient world was characterized by sophisticated societal collaborations in the absence of a sovereign state, or any other formal authority. Such spaces and organizational forms have become increasingly rare, however, as colonial control and capitalism's power spread across the globe (Hou, 2010).

Deresiewicz described the disappearance of affordable art space as an erasure whereby a community goes from *gritty* (usually a racist determination about the denizens) to *edgy* (newly bohemian) and finally to *vibrant* (meaning hipsters have taken over). Ask anyone who has been around Burning Man for a long time and they'll describe a similar Grit to Gentrified process. Whether it is possible to create and nurture autonomous zones that last over time is an important question, not the least for policymakers and community organizers. Copenhagen's Freetown Christiania has operated as an autonomous zone for longer than we've been alive, demonstrating that it is possible to cultivate and sustain autonomous zones. More should be done to foster the anarcho-artistic vibe that pulses through our communities, since they are a critical ingredient for free and collaborative spaces.

Rethink Our Values

Connective creativity requires us to value *membership* and *belonging* in a group focused on sharing resources and credit and joy. The false solidarities of online communities and consumer culture are insufficient to the task. We need to rediscover more communal social values, find new ways of making kin, and cocreate fresh modes of reciprocity, community, sharing, and solidarity. These are the opposite of the individuation that neoliberal capitalism encourages worldwide. We need more love, self-sacrifice, courage, risk, humility, solidaristic and sacrificial action, investment in community and commons, more open societies, open access, and open minds. These are not new values, they are very old, borne from our deep history living in small bands and telling stories over shared fires.

If this sounds desirable, we should mention that it is also difficult. Our experience starting an artist collective suggests that building community is not for the impatient. As we explored in the case study, it has taken us five years to go from a bunch of like-minded people working together on art to a group with a shared vision and collective identity invested in building community. Communities foster a sense of shared identity, a willingness to share burdens and risk, and a sense of trust. As a result, the process of building and maintaining community is a lot like building and maintaining any relationship – it takes intentional and regular relational work. The fruit is a sense of solidarity. This may seem nice in and of itself, but it is in fact vital, an antidote to the corrosive power of those neoliberal and consumeristic trends that alienate us one from another.

Again, we are reminded of Donna Haraway's invitation to reimagine *kinship* and to invest in an *ethics of care*. Haraway's guidance comes in the midst of what she refers to as the "Chthulucene" – an opportunity to shift from the human-centric implications of the Anthropocene, and invest in a more inclusive, inter-connected, and multispecies approach to understanding and living in the world.

Kinship and care represent old ways, and we would do well to learn from them. The status quo in the art world is the same as it is everywhere else: hone your personal brand, optimize your product-market fit, and sell like crazy. This is the message we are sending to school-aged children: eliminate what doesn't fit on a standardized test. This is the message we are sending to college graduates: optimize for the job market. And this is the message we're sending to markets: profit is more important than our ecosystems and communities.

The act of *creating kin* – fostering communities of care and compassion – is both an antidote to the harm caused by the status quo and an alternative to the zero-sum world it hallucinates. Many years ago, British Prime Minister Margaret Thatcher suggested that when it came to unchecked markets, *there is no alternative*. It is our job, we think, to prove her wrong.

Make Time

One of the biggest impediments to connective creativity is time. We must find ways to free people up to spend more time creatively, if that is something they are inclined to do. That's how we got started. Thinking back to the group we met in Section 3, Diane, Nate, Gordon, and Austin are all professors who have earned tenure, a status which allows them free time for additional exploration into fresh scholarly and artistic terrain. The pressure to publish is ever-present (this Element is evidence of that fact), but the pressure to create a particular brand, earn revenue, and sell our art is completely absent. We have had the luxury to spend time thinking creatively, and that luxury has benefited the larger community around us.

Most of us tend to spend our time in ways that are patterned by larger cultural norms and economic incentives. In America, where we live, markets play an ever-growing role in capturing our work hours as well as our downtime, as we work for employers and then unwind by scrolling through advertising-funded social media landscapes. As artist Jenny Odell argues in her critique of the capitalistic attention economy *How to Do Nothing* (2019), doing nothing requires privilege, but it should be a basic human right denied to no one. Similarly, no time is left for unbridled creativity, it seems, between the demands placed on us by the market and the opportunities offered to us on our screens.

Thus, freeing people up to connect creatively is a matter of rethinking our values, as described in the previous section. Freeing people up for connection is also a matter of rethinking how we spend our time, and rethinking our time involves rethinking finances and livelihood. We are writing from an America where the only thing rising faster than consumer costs is the rate of inequality. Few have the luxury of time to themselves, let alone time to share creating with others.

Economists have noticed this and have suggested the creation of a Guaranteed Basic Income (GBI) whereby every citizen in a country would be supported with cash assistance at a minimum level. In other words, everyone is guaranteed a basic income sufficient to care for their basic needs. After that, the thinking goes, people are freed up to really worry about whatever it is that they would prefer to worry about, or give up on worrying altogether.

Some have suggested this approach as a solution to poverty. Others have suggested it might just be what saves us all in the event superintelligence and social robots take all human jobs. In either case, removing the threat of penury just might free people up for activities they hadn't previously had time for.

The logic of the market and the reality of economic systems like America's leave many people with little leisure time. More just economic systems are likely to free more people up to do what we are best at: connecting and creating. Those are our twinned birthrights. Guaranteeing a basic income for everyone is only one possible way of freeing more people up to do what we are here to do.

We think that being freed from acute financial worry would afford more time for imagination and creativity. In a GBI world, of course, we'd be chuffed if people spent some of their time creating with others. This belief is born of experience. In many ways, the major characters in Section 3 were all underwritten by a very old form of GBI: academic tenure.

The Last Word

This Element is about creativity when people work together. In particular, we focus on artistic collaborations, but these lessons apply more broadly. Collectives and collaborations allow people to play, form bonds, and come up with ideas they might not have on their own. This alternative approach flies in the face of conventional art worlds focused on the creative control and status rewards of the solo artist. We believe that all humans are creative, while only some decide to adopt the identity of *Artist*. And anyway, larger systems, often involving norms, institutions, and markets, disincentivize cooperation and sharing.

Artistic collaborations and collectives emerge despite these odds. These exceptions to the solo and lead artist rule are the result of individuals' decisions, in pivotal moments, to behave differently. Collaborative work takes many forms, but across them all we see the importance of play and playfulness, resources and resourcefulness, and a commitment to sharing that leads to collective identity, and on from there, to community.

We believe these collective action outcomes are a collective good. As such, they should be encouraged through investments in supportive norms, hospitable spaces, and institutional resources.

All this would be a small footnote to a series of archipelagos that constitute a Maverick Art World, were it not for the disturbing fact that the world is at an inflection point. Ecological destruction and an uptick in violent conflict are stark reminders that we need better ideas. Loneliness and loss suggest we need one another more than ever before. Focusing on groups of people working together to imagine and create art is our modest contribution to finding ways to build solidarity for human flourishing, and beyond. The urgency of this invitation should be clear. As he reviewed this manuscript, our colleague Nate noted, about the importance of creativity:

> I have come to see creation, in many ways, as directly antithetical to "doom scrolling." Social media can create a sense of powerlessness: the world is fucked, everyone's' lives are better than yours . . . it's a shit-show of unsolvable problems. Creation, conversely, is a positive activity with (generally) finite solutions to finite problems. Whether the artifact created "stems the tide" of evil in the world is almost beside the point: the mere act itself stands in opposition to existential dread.

This Element has argued that the role of collaboration is too often overlooked in the arts. In fact, we think that what we're calling *connective creativity* is too often overlooked across society, from the kitchen to the boardroom. To address the pressing challenges facing society today, we must develop new ways to create and connect. Collective art is not a cure-all for ennui, social alienation, or political antagonism, but the lessons from this world can help us think about how to support creativity more broadly. If we want to prepare for dramatic change, if we want our societies to flourish, if we want to engage in the important work of healing and repair, then we simply must increase our capacity to imagine and create *together*.

Coda: Collaboration Beyond the Human

How does this advocacy for connective community line up with the emerging reality of artificial intelligence?

This Element focuses on the idea of *art as collective action*. The community and connection that comes from working together on a sculpture is a profoundly human endeavor. Art, for time out of mind, has been a human endeavor. We mix the pigments, we trim the brushes, we sketch the lines, we stack the stones, we cut the fabric. In short, we – humans – make the art.

A hoard of interlopers is upending our time-honored traditions. Of course, we're talking about "artificial intelligence," a clumsy term for clever programming that draws on the vast trove of humanity's past endeavors in order to produce something novel and new. Or to try.

With one eye on the social and artistic practice required to write this Element and another eye on the headlines, we have begun to wonder what all this means for us. For us as academics, for us as authors, and for us as artists. Each of these roles and their attendant activities – brokers of ideas, brokers of words, brokers of representations – are mimicked by increasingly powerful tools. And these tools are not the creation of other academics, authors, and artists, but by technologists narrowly focused on capturing market share.

Their massive models rely on hoovering up the copyrighted work of authors and artists without their consent, to build these models without consulting content creators, and to release the final product into a society that appears wholly unprepared for the experiment. So far, not so good. Looking forward, however, how might "artificial intelligence" impact our corner of the maverick art world? What follows are our preliminary thoughts.

As this Element makes clear, we are bullish on human connection. We have found ourselves being described as artists, not because we were trained in an MFA program to think and talk like artists, but because we set out to build art with other people. What's most important to us is community, not canon. We are interested in ideas that bring people together rather than set individuals apart. As a result, we have little interest in outsourcing to an artificial mind what could be done in relationship with others. Perhaps our art would be more canonically relevant if we asked an AI model to perform as an MFA-trained artist. Perhaps our final products would be more polished if it was built by robots, rather than fit together by the hundreds of volunteer hands we have relied on.

The product might be "better," but the process is clearly worse. And we are solving for process. Yet this avoids the central question: What does artificial intelligence have to do with our art practice?

We are of two minds on this. Austin believes that the capacity to nurture, connect, create, and discover is humanity's birthright. The world has been profoundly shaped – for better and for worse – by our desire to take novel action in the world. Seen from this perspective, the capacity for creativity is widespread, and barriers to artistic practice should be eliminated. *Art* is not just what critics and curators deem worthy. Seen in this light, then, new digital tools like Sora, Stable Diffusion, and Dall-E democratize the process of getting something out of our head and onto paper or onto a screen.

There is a similar increase in the tools needed to take these ideas from our mind and the screen and manifest them tangibly in the world. Digital printers ensure that a person's conversation with an AI about an idea can end up as a physical artifact hanging on a wall. And 3D printers increase the likelihood that a conversation about a physical object, a sculpture for example, might someday soon end up on a mantle or in a garden. It is possible that neither picture nor sculpture ends up in a gallery or is considered to be *art* by the critics. So what? New digital tools force the question of whether what we love most about art is the ability to create and enjoy or the ability to hoard value and signal status.

We love the idea that a single person can have an idea, chat with another (artificial) mind, produce a sketch, imagine a prototype, and then print out the product. We believe that process is a form of creativity.

But of course our focus is on *connective* creativity. We are far more interested in the process of building community than we are in the act of producing something critics will certify as having artistic merit. From this perspective, the process of creating art with machines leaves something to be desired. We're not opposed to it in theory, but we do believe that the practice of communal creation has additional benefits. In fact, it is possible that our collective comes up with ideas that are *less unique* than what a large language model might be able to come up with. We're fine with that. Our goal is to build community around the process of creating art. If there's any critical acclaim in it for us, we're happy to have it, but that isn't the goal.

We are speaking as maverick artists. What of integrated artists, and those whose careers and livelihoods depend on their work being taken seriously? Critics and collectors are crucial to the process of *being taken seriously*. What should be taken seriously in an art world increasingly populated by artificial minds (like Dall-E and Stable Diffusion) and artificial hands (like printers, 3D printers, and soon robots)? These are uncertain times for artists who make their living producing art, and our "democratizing creativity" argument might be philosophically compelling, but it doesn't sell paintings or pay the bills. There are early signs that the proliferation of easy and affordable tools for doing tasks like logo design and illustration are hitting piece-work artists hard, and there is every reason to believe this trend will continue to impact artists working on more complex media, including fine art photography, film, graphic design, commercial art and photography, and so forth.

What should be done? Tectonic shifts in trade and technology must be managed with care. To see what should be avoided one need look no further than the North American Free Trade Agreement (NAFTA). Negotiated by elites in Canada, Mexico, and the United States, NAFTA was supposed to usher in a new era of more efficient trade, with benefits to the consumer markets of each respective country.

Lots of time was spent planning how governments would interface and how markets would benefit. Less time was spent planning for the fact that this dramatic shift in trade policy would upend the lives of people working in affected industries, for example the automobile manufacturing industry in the American Midwest. Corporate profit cycles and human life cycles are dramatically different. Workers who lost manufacturing jobs while in their forties, for example, were not well-served by the piecemeal retraining programs on offer.

This approach can be contrasted with the Works Progress Association (WPA). As the Great Depression threatened the livelihoods of countless Americans, the WPA stepped in to subsidize artists. Federal Project Number One launched efforts like the Federal Writers' Project, Federal Theatre Project,

Federal Music Project, and the Federal Art Project, and at its peak kept as many as 40,000 people in employment. Spending what would now be $600 million dollars allowed Federal Project Number One to underwrite an expansion, and democratization, of the American art scene.

As new technologies threaten to disrupt the livelihoods of countless artists (and make the individuals running a handful of tech companies unbelievably rich), contemporary policymakers should take a note from the WPA. The alternative is a generation of artists abandoned by the market in much the same way a generation of industrial workers were abandoned by NAFTA.

There are many ideas in circulation about how to manage these transitions. The possibility that developments in artificial intelligence and robotics might make human labor – both blue collar and white collar alike – irrelevant has led some to advocate for the establishment of a GBI. Others have gone so far as to suggest that radical technological changes will free humans up from the need to work – we won't be losing our jobs, we will be gaining our lives back from the necessity of labor, from dependence on the *sweat of our brow*.[12] A world without work is, of course, a world full of opportunity to connect and create with others.

Far more time should be invested in imagining how technological changes can benefit everyone, rather than catastrophizing about what all could go wrong. Best, perhaps, is a balance between planning contingencies and imagining potentials.

Let's return to the question we started out with: *How does our advocacy for connective community line up with the emerging reality of artificial intelligence?*

Here it might be useful to explore our own experiments with new technology. Our collective, ArtBuilds, is actively wrestling with how to bring in AI as a partner that supports, rather than replaces, human creativity. In the fall of 2023, our team returned soaked and exhausted from the muddiest Burning Man on record.[13] While the rest of the group was busy attending to the parts of their lives they had neglected over the summer, Gordon was on sabbatical and volunteered to spearhead our next proposal. He was able to engage folks for quick feedback on the idea for the art, but nobody had any energy to actually help write the proposal and name the piece.

It was here that Gordon turned to ChatGPT for help. It was early days, so the process was surreal and addictive. Instead of waiting and waiting for an emailed response to his half-baked idea, Gordon received immediate and detailed

---

[12] Genesis 3:19.

[13] Contrary to the dire news reports at the time, it was the best Burning Man any of us have attended. We immediately began planning for next year, hence the need to submit another art proposal.

feedback. While that feedback wasn't perfect, it didn't need to be. The importance lay in the *process*, the back and forth between Gordon and ChatGPT, rather than in any single answer or solution set. Critically, Gordon did not simply ask ChatGPT a question and use its answer whole cloth. He instead engaged the AI in an iterative loop. They passed paragraphs back and forth, collaborating on the language until it landed somewhere that Gordon was happy with.

When we wrote this paragraph, the same thing occurred between our own two human minds, one drafting, one refining, one fixing, one replacing. Together we work *iteratively* in a process that leads to a fundamentally emergent final project. This is our second book together, so we have gotten good at bouncing ideas off of one another – testing, exploring, discarding, rediscovering.

Working in real time with an artificial mind helped Gordon to break the logjam of solitary thinking and get a halfway decent proposal drafted. In this way, slowly, in conversation with another mind, the narrative emerged. The resulting proposal didn't come from AI or from Gordon so much as it was the emergent property of the conversation. This process even extended to the project's title. After a few failed prompts that generated bland and stereotypical options, Gordon hit on the right sequence of prompts. He asked ChatGPT to generate a list of words combining the theme of the piece with one of his favorite authors:

Gordon: "Create a list of words David Foster Wallace would love related to shadows."

ChatGPT: "Obscurity, penumbra, murkiness, nuances, concealment, opacity, shadiness, ambiguity, chiaroscuro, intricacy, veiled, enigma, subtlety, mystery, dimness, penumbras, esoteric, profundity, concealment, twilight."

Penumbra caught Gordon's eye – it invokes edges and the unknown, but also a certain degree of promise. Gordon shared this impression with Diane, Nate, and Austin. We loved it, and the name stuck. Was it connective creativity? Absolutely. And it is not that different from how our minds can work as well. Austin, for example, talks to himself, and sometimes interviews himself, or tasks his mind with things to mull over while he's sleeping. It strikes us that Austin talking to himself and Gordon talking to an artificial mind are, at some level, analogous. It's the back-and-forth that is so valuable. Creativity is dialectical.

Austin liked this name as soon as he saw it. As ArtBuild's chief storyteller, Austin is usually tasked with describing our work. Over the years he has integrated his exploration of concepts related to structure, agency, process, relationality, emergence, and liminality (both temporal and spatial) into their work. In the shadow-edge of *penumbra* he saw parallels with the notion of the liminal, the in-between space and the in-between times. The narrative arc between the projects was coherent and was something Austin would build off of in his descriptions of this new work. Did ChatGPT know any of this? Of course not. But Gordon saw something in the suggested title. He knew David Foster Wallace would approve, and he was confident it would give Austin plenty of creative runway.

This vignette embodies what we see as the best possible role for other minds in the creative process. ChatGPT's role was catalytic – it was a nonhuman mind that jumpstarted our offline creativity. What's more, it was a human–nonhuman collaboration that served our human–human collaboration.

Using ChatGPT to help us name a piece was not controversial for our collective. The more we talked about using AI in our practice, however, the more our thinking has diverged. Some are of the mind that we should not involve AI at all in the process of concept generation. Even if the AI produces a superb idea, some of us would hate to have outsourced this part of the process to a nonhuman mind. A major reason for this resistance is that concept generation, rather than naming the piece, for example, is what excites people in our collective. Discussion and debate are an important part of what brought us together in the first place. If AI were to simply generate a great idea, then we would be short-circuiting a core component of what makes our collective a collective. The fear is that we may simply turn into a construction crew for AI-generated concepts.

Others, in contrast, are more bullish on AI and are interested in bringing it in as both a practical tool and a creative collaborator. By way of example, one member of the collective's personal artistic practice is entirely AI-driven. He has become extremely talented at writing prompts that generate thousands of potential images. He then painstakingly reviews each of these images to find the few that best capture what he is after. These then become input for another cycle of creative generation, leading to some remarkable and novel outputs. While this particular approach does not currently work well for sculpture, we have no doubt that the next few generations of AI will make it possible to produce coherent and physically realizable sculptural designs in the way that today's models render 2D images.

We, Austin and Gordon, are much more willing to experiment with disruptive technology. Our last project, remember, involved drones. This is primarily because we are very optimistic about human potential moving forward, and a little skeptical of the argument that creative ecosystems should be protected from disruption. From where we are sitting, the status quo gatekeeps what is deemed worthy, and the market is increasingly the metric whereby art markets are judged. This is particularly true as fine art has entered the bloodstream of financialized capital. Disrupting the status quo might not be so bad, so long as we can protect people embedded in the last dispensation, ideally in a way that provides financial support (hence our thinking about GBI and the WPA).

Perhaps this is why we're less worried about artificial minds replacing human minds in some creative endeavors. Imagine a writers' room for a television show composed of a single human and a team of AI chatbots. Do we want to live in that world? AI-written TV shows on Netflix, for example, have a host of downsides, including a lack of originality, lack of emotional depth, and a lack of artistic vision.

Our sense, however, is that each of these critiques can be leveled in various ways at Hollywood blockbusters, Bollywood in India, Nollywood in Nigeria, K-Dramas from Korea, procedural dramas, and any other creative sector where consistency is prioritized above novelty. In fact, Netflix has cornered the streaming industry by using huge tranches of viewership data to reverse-engineer the process of content creation. Gone is the artistic vision of the screenwriter or director, it has been largely replaced by formulas provided by the data boffins. Ask any screenwriter and director and they will tell you: the age of algorithms is already here. Netflix is, in a manner of speaking, behaving as an enterprise-scale GPT. And Hollywood is no better, spinning out sequels faster than anyone can watch them.

Human creativity has been so heavily filtered through financialized capital systems that our greatest gift is rendered unpalatable. Yet this is not a justification for undifferentiated content to instead come from AI, but instead a clarion call for humans to band together and create things that are unmistakably *human*. At the time of writing, BookToks have mobilized TikTok-addicted young people to rescue the legacy American bookseller Barnes and Noble from cultural and financial irrelevance. Physical books suddenly matter again. So do record players – their sales are at an all-time high.[14] People will still want things that have some heft, and when they want something light, perhaps we simply hand the Marvel and DC Comic intellectual property over to Sam Altman, and let his outfit spin out the drab sequels, thus freeing real humans up to do some real dreaming, to really pursue our artistic visions.

"Some heft," "real dreaming," "artistic vision," though, are socially constructed. An increase in cultural omnivorism means that an increasing number of people are consuming both "high-brow" and "low-brow" cultural products. Over time it is likely that a particular AI aesthetic will gain popularity in the

---

[14] Statistica. 2023. "Unit Sales of Turntables in the U.S. 2005–2021." Published by Statista Research Department, June 22, 2023. Available online at: www.statista.com/statistics/448555/number-of-turntables-sold-in-the-us.

same way the filters bundled with our smartphones emulates the way color film looks after a few years in the sun – the glitch of a chemical's half-life remade as an aesthetically desirable feature.

Perhaps we can now return to the original question: *How does our advocacy for connective community line up with the emerging reality of artificial intelligence?* Our thinking about the answer is built into our framing of the question. The common question *what will artificial intelligence do to creativity* misses the very thing we hold most important: connection and community. If this Coda offers any insight, it is the invitation to explore the interplay of these new tools with our ancient creative capacity to engage. This exploration must keep our highest aspirations in mind. For us, that highest aspiration is to create and commune with other humans, using whatever tools we have at our disposal.

Appendix: Methods

We wrote this Element in an attempt to better understand our own experience starting an art collective. Back in 2019, we had no hypothesis about connective creativity, we just wanted to build art with our friends: Diane Hoffoss, Nate Parde, and hundreds of collaborators and volunteers. Over time, that desire to build art has resulted in founding of the nonprofit, ArtBuilds Collective Ltd., and in experiences ranging from self-funded projects to commissioned installations alongside teams as small as 7 to installations requiring well over 100 volunteers.

This project also draws on original research in two forms. We have, between the two of us, engaged in more than 130 months of continuous autoethnographic fieldwork. Austin wrote a case study of ArtBuilds, which involved interviews with all key participants, including Gordon.

Gordon conducted semi-structured interviews with twenty-one people in nine collaborative groups. Our interview questions drew on our experience with ArtBuilds. *What's the relationship between artistic identity and the market? Who gets to call themselves an "artist"? Why do people join a project if nobody's name is going to be on the art? Who gets credit for a design? Who gets to talk about what the piece "means"?*

This Element draws heavily on our own research and experience, but we have learned a lot from others. Imre Szeman, for example, has used the Oil School convenings to collectively author a book. The Sunlight Foundation, for example, brings people together to talk and think and write about daylight. Austin is experimenting with these approaches in a working group at Yale University focused on the future of exploitation and emancipation. In their own way, each of these efforts experiment with different resources, norms, spaces, and institutions.

References

Abraham, Anna. (2018). *The Neuroscience of Creativity*. Cambridge: Cambridge University Press.

Abraham, Anna, ed. (2020). *The Cambridge Handbook of the Imagination*. Cambridge: Cambridge University Press.

Anderson, Benedict. (1983). *Imagined Communities*. New York: Verso.

Bayles, David, and Ted Orland. (2001). *Art & Fear: Observations on the Perils (and Rewards) of Artmaking*. Santa Cruz, CA: Image Continuum Press.

Becker, Howard S. (2008). *Art Worlds: Updated and Expanded*. Berkeley: University of California Press.

Bey, Hakim. (2003). *TAZ: The Temporary Autonomous Zone, Ontological Anarchy, Poetic Terrorism*. New York: Autonomedia.

Bishop, Claire. (2012). *Artificial Hells: Participatory Art and the Politics of Spectatorship*. New York: Verso Books.

Bourdieu, Pierre. (1984). *Distinction: A Social Critique of the Judgement of Taste*. Cambridge, MA: Harvard University Press.

Brown, Kate. (2023). Art Collectives Were the Talk of the Art World in the Last Few Years: Has Their Moment Passed? *ArtNet*. https://news.artnet.com/art-world-archives/art-collectives-2252767.

Buber, Martin. (1970). *I and Thou*. New York: Simon and Schuster.

Cameron, Julia. (2022). *The Artist's Way: 30th Anniversary Edition*. New York: Penguin.

Chen, Kathryn K. (2009). *Enabling Creative Chaos: The Organization behind the Burning Man Event*. Chicago, IL: University of Chicago Press.

Choi-Fitzpatrick, Austin. (2020). *The Good Drone: How Social Movements Democratize Surveillance*. Cambridge, MA: MIT Press.

Choi-Fitzpatrick, Austin. (2024). Disruption and Emergence: How to Think about Human Rights Futures. *Journal of Human Rights*, 23(1), 105–123.

Choi-Fitzpatrick, Austin, and Amelia Watkins-Smith. (2021). Agency Continuum? A Non-binary Approach to Agency among Human Rights Victims and Violators. *Human Rights Quarterly*, 43(4), 714–735.

Choi-Fitzpatrick, Austin, Douglas Irvin-Erickson, and Ernesto Verdeja, eds. (2022). *Wicked Problems: The Ethics of Action for Peace, Rights, and Justice*. New York: Oxford University Press.

Christo and Jeanne-Claude. (nd). *Wrapped Reichstag*. Accessed August 7, 2024. https://christojeanneclaude.net/artworks/wrapped-reichstag/.

Collins, Randall. (1998). *The Sociology of Philosophies: A Global Theory of Intellectual Change*. Cambridge, MA: Belknap Press of Harvard University Press.

Crewdson, Gregory. (2008). Gregory Crewdson – Close Up – Ovation. YouTube, accessed online in February 2024 at https://youtu.be/RywAfP4KFcY?si=ByFtFYWhkiIrj2tX).

Csikszentmihalyi, Mihaly. (1990). *Flow: The Psychology of Optimal Experience*. New York: Harper & Row.

De Wachter, Ellen Mara. (2017). *Co-art: Artists on Creative Collaboration*. London: Phaidon.

Deresiewicz, William. (2020). *The Death of the Artist: How Creators Are Struggling to Survive in the Age of Billionaires and Big Tech*. New York: Henry Holt.

Edmondson, A. (1999). Psychological Safety and Learning Behavior in Work Teams. *Administrative Science Quarterly*, 44(2), 350–383.

Emirbayer, Mustafa. (1997). Manifesto for a Relational Sociology. *American Journal of Sociology*, 103(2), 281–317.

Emirbayer, Mustafa, and Matthew Desmond. (2015). *The Racial Order*. Chicago, IL: University of Chicago Press.

Farrell, Michael. (2008). Comment on Neil McLaughlin: Types of Creativity and Types of Collaborative Circles: New Directions for Research. *Sociologica*, 2(2), 1–9.

Farrell, Michael P. (2001). *Collaborative Circles: Friendship Dynamics and Creative Work*. Chicago, IL: University of Chicago Press.

Fields, Ziska. (2021). Evaluating Collective and Creative Problem-Solving Approaches and Tools for Wicked Problems. In Fields, Z., ed., *Handbook of Research on Using Global Collective Intelligence and Creativity to Solve Wicked Problems*. Hershey, PA: IGI Global, pp. 41–68.

Fine, Gary Alan. (1979). Small Groups and Culture Creation: The Idioculture of Little League Baseball Teams. *American Sociological Review*, 44(5), 733–745.

Fine, Gary Alan. (2012). *Tiny Publics: A Theory of Group Action and Culture*. New York: Russell Sage Foundation.

Fine, Gary Alan. (2018). *Talking Art: The Culture of Practice and the Practice of Culture in MFA Education*. Chicago, IL: University of Chicago Press.

Fischer, Gerhard, and Florian Vassen, eds. (2011). *Collective Creativity: Collaborative Work in the Sciences, Literature and the Arts*. Vol. 148. London: Brill.

Foucault, Michels. (1984). What Is an Author? In Rabinow, P., ed., *The Foucault Reader*. New York: Pantheon Books, pp. 101–120.

Graeber, David, and David Wengrow. (2021). *The Dawn of Everything: A New History of Humanity*. London: Penguin.

Grant, Daniel. (2016). Social Practice Degrees Take Art to a Communal Level. *The New York Times*. www.nytimes.com/2016/02/07/education/edlife/social-practice-degrees-take-art-to-a-communal-level.html#:~:text=They%20view%20art%20as%20solitary,poor%20and%20victims%20of%20violence.

Haraway, Donna J. (2020). *Staying with the Trouble: Making Kin in the Chthulucene*. Durham, NC: Duke University Press.

Harvey, David. (2015). *The Right to the City*. In LeGates, R., and Stout, F., eds., *The City Reader*. New York: Routledge, pp. 314–322.

Helguera, Pablo. (2012). *Education for Socially Engaged Art*. New York: Jorge Pinto Books.

Hoople, Gordon, and Austin Choi-Fitzpatrick. (2020). *Drones for Good: How to Bring Sociotechnical Thinking into the Classroom*. New York: Springer.

Hou, Jeffrey, ed. (2010). *Insurgent Public Space: Guerrilla Urbanism and the Remaking of Contemporary Cities*. New York: Routledge.

Kahneman, Daniel. (2011). *Thinking, Fast and Slow*. New York: Macmillan.

Kelley, Tom, and David Kelley. (2013). *Creative Confidence: Unleashing the Creative Potential within Us All*. New York: Currency.

Lena, Jennifer C. (2019). *Entitled: Discriminating Tastes and the Expansion of the Arts*. Princeton, NJ: Princeton University Press.

Massenkoff, Maxim, and Nathan Wilmers. (2023). Rubbing Shoulders: Class Segregation in Daily Activities. SSRN, http://dx.doi.org/10.2139/ssrn.4516850.

McAdam, Doug. (1999). *Political Process and the Development of Black Insurgency, 1930-1970*. Chicago, IL: University of Chicago Press.

Mead, Rebecca. (2022). Anish Kapoor's Material Values. *New Yorker*, www.newyorker.com/magazine/2022/08/22/anish-kapoors-material-values.

Mulgan, Geoff. (2023). *Prophets at a Tangent: How Art Shapes Social Imagination*. Cambridge: Cambridge University Press.

Nussbaum, Martha C. (1998). *Cultivating Humanity*. Cambridge, MA: Harvard University Press.

Nussbaum, Martha C. (2006). *Frontiers of Justice: Disability, Nationality, Species Membership*. Cambridge, MA: Harvard University Press.

Odell, Jenny. (2019). *How to Do Nothing: Resisting the Attention Economy*. New York: Melville House.

Putnam, Robert D. (2000). *Bowling Alone: The Collapse and Revival of American Community*. New York: Simon and Schuster.

Rochon, Thomas R. (1998). *Culture Moves: Ideas, Activism, and Changing Values*. Princeton, NJ: Princeton University Press.

Schneider, Katy, and Adriane Quinlan. (2023). Tom Sachs Promised a Fun Cult: The Sculptor Likes to Call His Studio Part of His Art Practice: Working There Could Often Be Scary. *Curbed*, www.curbed.com/article/tom-sachs-studio-employees-office-culture.html.

Scott, James C. (2012). *Two Cheers for Anarchism: Six Easy Pieces on Autonomy, Dignity, and Meaningful Work and Play.* Princeton, NJ: Princeton University Press.

Shirky, Clay. (2008). *Here Comes Everybody: The Power of Organizing without Organizations*. New York: Penguin.

Simmel, Georg. (2009). *Sociology: Inquiries into the Construction of Social Forms*. Boston, MA: Brill.

Stavrides, Stavros. (2016). *Common Space: The City as Commons*. London: Bloomsbury.

Stimson, Blake, and Gregory Sholette, eds. (2007). *Collectivism after Modernism: The Art of Social Imagination after 1945*. Minneapolis: University of Minnesota Press.

Thompson, Nato. (2012). *Living as Form, Socially Engaged Art from 1991–2011*. Cambridge, MA: MIT Press.

Unger, Roberto Mangabeira. (2007). *The Self Awakened: Pragmatism Unbound*. Cambridge, MA: Harvard University Press.

Weeks, J. (2004). The Poincaré dodecahedral Space and the Mystery of the Missing Fluctuations. *Notices of the AMS*, 51(6), 610–619.

Wohl, Hannah. (2021). *Bound by Creativity: How Contemporary Art Is Created and Judged*. Chicago, IL: University of Chicago Press.

Zuboff, Shoshana. (2018). *The Age of Surveillance Capitalism: The Fight for a Human Future at the New Frontier of Power*. New York: Public Affairs.

Acknowledgments

We are extremely grateful to everyone in ArtBuilds – especially coconspirators Diane Hoffoss and Nate Parde – for their camaraderie. We are also thankful to the many folks who helped make this project possible: artists we interviewed, photographers who shared their images (especially Frank Guthrie), fellow travelers (Satyan Devadoss), and folks who took the time to discuss this project with us (including Bayo Akomolafe, Caroline Baille, Jon Bialecki, Andrew Biros, Jessica Buell, Janice Deaton, Philip Gamaghelyan, Sarah Howard, Daniel Leonard, Geoff Moran, Anna Mae Duane, Robert Valiente-Neighbours, Brandon Viadyanathan, Zoya Sardashti, Cortney Siegel, Dexter Pratt, and two anonymous reviewers). Austin's work on this project was supported by the Aspen Institute, through a Scholar in Residence fellowship in the Aspen Global Leadership Network.

At the University of San Diego we would like to thank the Deans who have supported our work, including Patricia Marquez and Darren Kew (Deans of the Kroc Peace School), Chell Roberts (Dean of the Shiley School of Engineering), and Noelle Norton (Dean of the College of Arts and Sciences). The donors who made our art possible include the Burning Man Project, the City of San Diego, San Diego Collaborative Art Project, the University of San Diego, Colin and MJ of Glass House Arts, and hundreds of individual donors who have been so generous with their time, their money, or both. We are especially grateful to the hundreds of students and community members who have made this connective creativity possible.

About the Authors

Austin Choi-Fitzpatrick is a cofounder of the California-based collective *ArtBuilds*. Recent installations have been commissioned by Burning Man and the City of San Diego, and include *About Time* (2019), *Emergence* (2020), *Reflexion* (2022), *Re:Emergence* (2022), *Unfolding Humanity* (2023), and *Penumbra* (2024). At the University of San Diego, he serves as Associate Provost (of Academic Strategy and Growth), Professor (of Sociology at the Kroc School), and Faculty Director (of the Institute for Social Innovation). He is concurrently a scholar-in-residence at the Aspen Institute's Global Leadership Network, and a visiting scholar at Yale University, where he codirects the GLC Future of Slavery and Emancipation Working Group.

Gordon Hoople is an artist, engineer, and educator. He cofounded *ArtBuilds*, a collective that creates large format participatory sculpture installations designed to make people stop, smile, and engage. He is also a founding faculty member and an associate professor with the Integrated Engineering Department at the University of San Diego. There he prepares students to tackle the world's most complicated problems with an eye towards designing a sustainable future. He is an award-winning educator whose NSF-funded research develops pedagogies that help students and faculty develop a critical understanding of the ways engineers impact society. Gordon received the PhD degree in mechanical engineering from UC Berkeley. *Art as Collective Action* is Austin and Gordon's second book together. Find him online at hoople.me.

Creativity and Imagination

Anna Abraham

University of Georgia, USA

Anna Abraham, Ph.D. is the E. Paul Torrance Professor at the University of Georgia, USA. Her educational and professional training has been within the disciplines of psychology and neuroscience, and she has worked across a diverse range of academic departments and institutions the world over, all of which have informed her cross-cultural and multidisciplinary focus. She has penned numerous publications including the 2018 book, *The Neuroscience of Creativity* (Cambridge University Press), and 2020 edited volume, *The Cambridge Handbook of the Imagination*. Her latest book is *The Creative Brain: Myths and Truths* (2024, MIT Press).

About the Series

Made in the USA
Monee, IL
07 July 2026

56550163R10046